*S*pirits
Between the Bays
Series

Volume VI

Crying
in the
Kitchen

STORIES OF Ghosts THAT ROAM THE WATER

Ed Okonowicz

Myst and Lace Publishers, Inc.

Spirits Between the Bays
Volume VI
Crying in the Kitchen
First Edition

Copyright 1998 by Edward M. Okonowicz Jr.
All rights reserved.

ISBN 0-9643244-8-2

Published by
Myst and Lace Publishers, Inc.
1386 Fair Hill Lane
Elkton, Maryland 21921

Printed in the U.S.A.
by Modern Press

Artwork, Typography and Design
by Kathleen Okonowicz

Dedications

In memory of the priests at Salesianum School,
from whom I learned so much, particularly Rev. John T. Spragg
Ed Okonowicz

To Joyce Buker, my aunt.
You are a wonderful person. I love you very much.
Kathleen Burgoon Okonowicz

Acknowledgments

The author and illustrator appreciate the assistance of those
who have played an important role in this project.

Special thanks are extended to

Paul Arbogast, Alicia Bjornson, Hazel D. Brittingham, Ruth Citro,
Rorie Dean, Mike Dixon, Jennings Evans,
Lisa Harrision and Ashley Biscoe, Lee Jennings, Ruth Jones,
Carleen Lewandowski, David Quillen, Larry Sharp,
Wanda Somers, Patrice Swadey and Lorie Whissel

for their assistance;

and to

John Brennan
Barbara Burgoon
Sue Moncure
Ted Stegura and
Monica Witkowski
for their proofreading and suggestions;

and, of course,

particular appreciation to the ghosts and their hosts.

Also available from Myst and Lace Publishers, Inc.

Spirits Between the Bays Series

Volume I
Pulling Back the Curtain
(October, 1994)

Volume II
Opening the Door
(March, 1995)

Volume III
Welcome Inn
(September, 1995)

Volume IV
In the Vestibule
(August, 1996)

Volume V
Presence in the Parlor
(April, 1997)

Volume VI
Crying in the Kitchen
(April, 1998)

Stairway over the Brandywine
A Love Story
(February, 1995)

Possessed Possessions
Haunted Antiques, Furniture and Collectibles
(March, 1996)

Disappearing Delmarva
Portraits of the Peninsula People
(August, 1997)

FIRED!
A DelMarVa Murder Mystery
(May, 1998)

Table of Contents

Legend and Lore

✴ These individuals have allowed real names and actual locations to be used in this presentation of their story.

   Site is open to the public

Introduction

In this, our sixth volume of the *Spirits Between the Bays* ghost series, we meet in the kitchen of our haunted house to share ghost stories from sites specifically related to water.

Good friends, relatives and neighbors rarely enter through the front door of a home. That formal setting is reserved for special holiday occasions and the infrequent arrival of special guests. The side of the house or back kitchen door is the comfortable, expected entrance reserved for our regulars. It's around the old kitchen table—with coffee brewing and the aroma of baking or, better yet, fresh scrapple—that our most secret experiences are shared.

Relaxed in this familiar spot, we talk of life and love, of death and mystery, and of course, of things that go bump in the night. In the kitchen we confess our sins, share our secrets and spin our yarns. It's there, for generations, that stories have been passed down to the young.

This volume belongs to our coast ghosts, those eerie spirits in the watertowns and beach villages. These tales came from workers on Pea Patch Island in Delaware, and from residents of Salem and Cape May in New Jersey, from Conowingo and Smith Island in Maryland, from Chincoteague in Virginia, and from the seaport of Lewes, perhaps Delaware's most haunted town.

While listening to these stories in the early evening, I heard the sound of the ocean invading the land. As shadows began to lengthen when the sun fell father behind the horizon, I imagined the unseen creatures that lurk beneath the sea, or others who live in the marshes, wetlands and near river beds.

Sailors say that man is not meant to be buried at sea. It's in the earth that he should rest for eternity. Many believe those who enter a watery grave do not stay put. Such spirits are forced to roam the ocean bottom and ride the waves, forever seeking the shore.

1

After washing up on the sandy wetlands, these restless souls yearn for the shelter of the dark ground, and some may reach out desperately to the living for help in reaching eternal rest.

Who's to say whether the theory is right or wrong?

More than once I've stood at the shoreline at night, alone, staring at the distant lights that blink in the blackness. I'm sure I've seen movement, heard muted whispers, smelled something nearby . . . only to turn and see vast stretches of empty sand and hear the steady rhythm of the crashing waves.

But, was something there? The walking dead, perhaps, seeking a shoreside grave or sandy pit in which to rest.

One reader suggested that DelMarVa has a large number of ghosts because phantoms cannot get off the peninsula, cannot travel across water, as the old superstition says.

It's an interesting suggestion. I don't know if water has ever stopped a persistent spirit.

In these pages you will meet unsettled souls, both kind and evil. Keep in mind that they do exist. These are not fairy tales or campfire stories to scare scouts into staying close to their cabins after dark. The people who have shared their experiences know what occurred. And, if you are in the right place at the right time, you, too, might be touched by a shadow from the unknown.

Until we meet again in **FIRED!**; ***Possessed Possessions 2: More Haunted Antiques, Furniture and Collectibles***; and **Vol. VII, *Up the Back Stairway* . . . .**

Sleep With the Light On and Happy Hauntings,

—Ed Okonowicz
in Fair Hill, Maryland,
at the northern edge
of the Delmarva Peninsula
—Spring 1998

Angelic Ghost of Cape May

I n April of 1976, the entire seaside town of Cape May, New Jersey, was named a National Historic Landmark. With more than 600 Victorian-era structures standing in the town today, it's difficult for visitors to grasp even a fraction of the decorated architectural detail on the rows of homes, shops, hotels and inns. Pastel porches, towering turrets, gingerbread gables and twisted trim compete for the observer's eye.

Cape May has been a resort area since the 1760s, even before the United States was a country. After a fire destroyed much of the center of town in 1878, many of the current day Victorian structures were built. Then, following a major hurricane in March 1962, the town again made a comeback by restoring its damaged homes. Therefore, the town's current appearance is due in large part to the community's efforts following two major disasters.

Ghost readers know that during the Victorian period ghost stories were even more popular than they are today. So, shouldn't Cape May harbor its fair share of ghosts and legends?

The answer is "Yes!"

One of the town's most fascinating haunted sites, and the source of hundreds of ghostly incidents, is the Angel of the Sea Bed and Breakfast, located on Trenton Avenue, a mere half-block from Beach Drive and the Atlantic Ocean.

The History

The history of the inn's two buildings is closely associated with the antics of one of the inn's most active ghosts.

According to a brief chapter in the *Angel of the Sea Cookbook*, the two buildings were constructed about 1850 as a "summer cottage" for William Weightman Sr., a Philadelphia chemist who discovered and manufactured quinine water for medicinal purposes.

But, it was originally built as a single structure at the corner of Franklin and Washington streets, where the Cape May Post Office currently stands. In 1881, Weightman's son decided he wanted an ocean view for his family and guests who often sat on the broad porches. He hired local farmers to "move" the house to the corner of Ocean and Beach avenues, the present site of the Marquis de Lafayette hotel.

The farmers discovered the house was too large to move as one unit. Not wanting to lose the winter work, they cut the building in half and moved it in sections, planning to reconnect the structure after the move.

It took the workers the entire winter to pull the sections on rolling tree trunks using mule and horse power. However, when they arrived at the new location, they found that while the livestock were well suited for "pulling" the house, they were incapable of "pushing" it back together. To complete the job they sealed up the sides and set the new two cottages in place. Over the next several decades the two buildings also served as a guest house, hotel and restaurant.

In 1962, the two-building unit was purchased by Rev. Carl McIntire and moved to its present site, this time on flatbed trucks. From 1962 to 1981, the houses were used to board employees from several nearby inns and as a dormitory for students from Shelton College, a religious school in the area.

From 1981 through 1988, the building was abandoned. The next owners, builder and developer John Girton, and his wife, Barbara, renovated the two structures, spending approximately $3.5 million. The first of the two buildings opened in July 1989, and the other section opened a year later.

Since that time, the inn has earned a national reputation for providing the highest quality service in an atmosphere of Victorian elegance, and there also have been the stories about its resident ghosts.

The Haunts

When I was beginning to write *Welcome Inn* in the summer of 1995, I began calling area hotels, restaurants, museums and inns to see if any of them had a "haunted room." One of my earliest calls was to the Angel of the Sea.

I still remember the conversation.

"Hi," I said, a bit apprehensively. "I'd like to ask you a strange question. Do you have any ghosts in your inn?"

Without hesitation, the person on the other end of the line said, quite casually, "Yes! Would you like to stay in the ghost room?"

At the time, I wasn't looking for stories too far beyond the boundaries of Delmarva, but I knew that someday I would get to the Angel of the Sea.

In the spring of 1997, I was at a book signing at Barnes & Noble in Bel Air, Maryland. During the discussion of *Presence in the Parlor*, a lady named Pamela asked if I had ever heard anything about ghosts in the Angel of the Sea.

After telling her it was on my "to visit" list, she shared her haunted experience. Afterwards, I made definite plans to conduct a series of on-site interviews.

Pamela told all of us in the bookstore that she had taken her niece to the beach during the summer for a brief getaway. In the middle of the night, they both were awakened by the movement of their bed.

At first, Pamela thought, *That's nice, a vibrating bed*. Soon, she realized that it was more than that. The bed was actually shaking. She tried to remain calm and told her niece it probably was vibration caused from a back-up generator used by the inn for emergency power.

"I also was worried," Pamela said. "It was the first time I had taken my niece away for a trip, and I didn't want my sister to be upset with me if anything went wrong."

Pamela said she went to the main desk the next morning and asked the hostess if the building was haunted.

Finding out there were spirited reports in the inn didn't help matters, especially since there was no vacancy and Pamela and her niece couldn't be moved into another room.

When the vibration happened the second night, Pamela said she got angry and shouted at whatever it was to "Stop it!"

Whatever it was responded, and the bed stopped moving. But, apparently Pamela and her niece continued shaking until they left the inn.

When I interviewed Bridget Fowler, the inn's manager and "cruise director" since 1989, on a warm January afternoon in 1998, she immediately recalled the story of the shaking bed—along with hundreds of other mini-incidents that, she said, "happen all the time."

Primarily there is the "swaying" of furniture, televisions turning on by themselves, lights going on and doors being unlocked.

But these have to do with the ghost in the "other building," the one located father away from the beach.

The source of the activity seems to be a young girl who was lodging in a room in the "other building" in the 1960s. The story states that a teenage girl, who was employed at the Christian Admiral Hotel (that has since been torn down), rushed back to her room to clean up before she went to a nearby church service.

Unfortunately, she had misplaced her key or left it at work. Rather than returning to the Christian Admiral and apparently deciding not to seek the assistance of the housekeeper, she climbed the fire escape or crawled out the hallway window—no one is sure. Balanced on the narrow third-floor ledge, she tried to get into her room through the window.

The wooden window gave way easily, but the bulky screen—which apparently was on the inside of the window frame—was more difficult. As she tried to pry it open, the screen snapped loose, causing the girl to lose her balance and fall backwards onto the ground below.

She was discovered, sitting in an upright position between the two buildings, dead.

The girl's name was never known, Bridget said, until a visitor came to the Angel of the Sea. The man explained that he had seen the story of the inn on The Learning Channel's *Great Country Inns* in 1992. At the time of the girl's death, the man said he and his father managed the Christian Admiral Hotel, and he said that he knew the girl and her last name was Brown.

Bridget, who also gives tours of the inn, said there are a number of rooms that are move active than others. She considers the ghostly "Miss Brown" to be pesky as opposed to horrifying. The teenage spirit is believed to be responsible for hauntings in the "other building."

"She has opened and closed doors," Bridget said. "She likes to watch TV, since she turns them on, not off. She doesn't like the dark, so she turns on the lights. And she doesn't like crowds, since she seems to be more prevalent when there are fewer people in the inn. But, she hasn't been as active since they tore down the Christian Admiral in 1996."

In the main building, whose parlor serves as the check-in site for all guests, other phantoms roam. That seems to be the theory of Lorie Whissel. She and her husband, Greg, are present owners of the inn.

"I think there are definitely more things happening over here," Lorie said. Without effort, she recited a litany of experiences that she and her relatives and employees had experienced, such as:

• The time she was pushed from the kitchen into the pantry,

• When the ghost pulled the front of her sweater up to her neck as she was speaking on the phone,

• The night all the furniture in one of the rooms was picked up and moved four inches away from the wall,

• The toilets that flush by themselves,

• The day something unseen tapped her on the shoulder,

• The times certain ceiling fans turned on by themselves,

• The night she and Greg were trying to sleep as the sound of whistling wind swirled around the room,

• The dark silhouette that appeared at the foot of a bed and

• The woman's figure that looks out at the parking lot from the kitchen window as employees arrive.

"When I was pregnant, both times, she harassed me non-stop," Lorie said. "That's when she pushed me. I used to talk to her a lot, but not after I was expecting. So I didn't give the ghost as much attention. That's what I think she wants, attention. I don't think she, I call it a she, is evil or menacing.

"I feel there are two entities here," Lorie said. "The documented girl in the other house is a trickster. The one here wants attention."

On this particular winter day, everyone seemed to have a ghost story. Holly, a chambermaid, recalled the day in the other house when she had completed fixing the mosquito netting and cleaning the room.

"I came back about an hour later, and I was the only one in the building that day," she said, "and the wind was blowing and the fan was turned on full blast."

Front desk manager Sharon Falkowski said she has had a few experiences. One occurred in the other building, but she actually saw a ghost in the main building.

While taking a couple on a tour of rooms in the building of the teenage ghost, Sharon said she tried the door handle of a room that was locked. She left the people standing in the hall and, within two minutes, returned with the key. But, when she came back and put her hand on the door handle the door opened.

"No one came and opened it while I was gone," she said. "The people were standing right there. They looked at me, and I looked at them. They asked me, 'Is this place haunted?'

"I said, 'No!' I didn't want them to get freaked out."

It was near the parlor in the main building where Sharon saw the ghost lady. Standing at the same site— beneath the first-floor archway and looking across the dining room—she pointed toward the rear of the building.

"I saw a reflection in the glass doors of the china cabinet," she said. "There was a figure, standing directly behind me, just to my left. It was so real that I turned to say, 'Can I help you?' and it was gone. There was nothing there.

"I turned to Bridget and said, 'I just saw the ghost!' All the experiences next door are sounds or things moving, but in this house people actually have seen something, like the lady at the kitchen window.

"I don't mind hearing about it when it has to do with some-one else," Sharon said. "Things like that don't bother me. But when it was standing right behind me, that scared me a bit."

Lorie and Bridget said most people passing through the Angel of the Sea don't notice much of the minor spirited activi-ties. And, in cases where they do, they don't connect it with a haunting.

"Sometimes, where they are leaving," Bridget said, "they might mention that their bed seemed to be shaking, or the TV went on by itself. They'll say, 'By the way, I kept finding my lipstick or my hairbrush on the floor, and I know I left it on the dresser.' Little things like that. Nothing major.

"We don't make a big thing about our ghosts," Bridget added, "and we don't give out the room numbers unless someone asks. That's because we've found that about 50 percent of people are afraid and the other 50 percent are intrigued. But I like the idea that we have someone here. It makes for interesting conversation. I tell them the story and they are fascinated."

Lorie added, "I like it a lot, and I like to talk to people about it. My father had an unusual experience once, and I saw a ghost in Austria. Our whole family must be on a psychic plane where we can see things like this."

Features: Throughout the year the two structures are adorned with the glow of 5,000 white, Christmas-style lights. Victorian-era elegance is apparent throughout. Period furnishings in all 27 guest rooms, each with a private bath. Full breakfast served. Afternoon tea time and evening wine and cheese. Magnificent parlor area with ornate fireplace and wood ceiling. Recognized as one of the top Ten B & Bs in the United States. Award winner from the National Trust for Historic Preservation in Washington, D.C. Has been featured on NBC, CBS, ABC, QVC and PBS, The Learning Channel, Discovery, *Good Morning America* and Oprah Winfrey's "Best Vacations in the World." Also named "Best Seaside Inn in the USA" and rated as one of the top two B & Bs in North America.

Sightings/Activity: At the back kitchen window facing the parking lot. In the kitchen near the pantry. At the archway, where the parlor meets the dining room. In several guest rooms in each building. However, the inn does not advertise the exact room number. If you desire to stay in a ghost room, ask when you make your reservation.

Contact: Open year round. 5-7 Trenton Avenue, Cape May, New Jersey 08204; telephone, (609) 884-3331. Web site: http://www.angelofthesea.com

Illustration courtesy of the Angel of the Sea

Lewes, Delaware's Most Haunted Town?

L ewes, the picturesque Delmarva seacoast town, is as rich in legend and lore as it is in history. It was in 1631—along the coast where the Delaware Bay meets the Atlantic Ocean—that the first European settlement was established in what would become part of Pennsylvania's lower three counties. But the small village didn't last long.

Indian Massacre

American Indians killed off the three dozen Dutch settlers within the first few months, and several decades passed before a permanent settlement was established in Lewes in 1658.

No doubt the sudden death of the murdered settlers generated a few roaming spirits, some who may still be in search of eternal rest. But the Swanendael Massacre was only the first of several documented tragedies and unusual events that have occurred in and near the Sussex County seacoast town.

Pirate Rest Stop

In the heyday of piracy (from the late 1600s until about 1750) the Atlantic port, then known as Lewestown, was recognized by government authorities and locals as a well-known watering hole for a large number of pirates. Among the unsavory visitors were such famous historical picaroons as Edward Teach (more often referred to as Blackbeard) and Captain William Kidd.

Blackbeard—who was spotted along the Delaware River frequently in the early 18th century—is said to have walked the cobblestones of New Castle, Delaware, and also spent a fair amount of time in Marcus Hook, Pennsylvania. In that Pennsylvania border town, the tall, menacing pirate and other buccaneers visited gin mills and hangouts on Discord Lane. The notorious alleyway received its name because of the many brawls, murders and crimes that took place at the site.

The area of Blackbird, Delaware, north of Smyrna, is believed to have been named after Blackbeard. That's partly because the pirate is reported to have hidden from authorities in its inlets, established several forts in the marshes and buried a fair share of ill-gotten treasure in the coastal wetlands. Amateur and professional prospectors still explore the area, many with sophisticated metal detectors. At least one treasure hunter has employed satellite imagery maps to help him in his continuing quest for Blackbeard's gold.

In one documented account related to Captain Kidd, one of his ships anchored in Lewestown harbor, and several town residents boarded the craft and purchased goods from the buccaneer. This was against the law. According to author Jack Beach in his fascinating book, *Pirates on the Delaware*, William Penn himself ordered that the citizens be arrested for consorting with the sea dog.

Kitts Hummock, a small community—located on the Delaware River just south of the Dover Air Force Base—is believed to have been named in honor of Captain Kidd.

Both Kidd and Teach are said to have buried numerous treasure chests containing gold, silver, copper pieces, precious stones and other bejeweled valuables beneath the sand along the Delaware, Maryland and New Jersey coasts.

With each precious fortune, however, it was the custom of pirate leaders to leave one of their crew behind—permanently—to guard the riches for all eternity. Bad luck and ill health are said to haunt anyone who disturbs the resting place of the pirate skeleton that rests atop each bulging treasure chest.

When the moon is full in Lewes, some say a phantom ship appears in the mist, and its hull can be seen floating in the waters of Lewes Creek. The glowing, light-colored outline is the ship of Blackbeard or Captain Kidd, coming back to pick up the buried booty that was left behind on the coast.

The H.M.S. DeBraak

Over hundreds of years, the Delaware Coast has witnessed thousands of shipwrecks. In summer storms and winter gales, both wooden sloops and iron ships have disappeared from sight and settled on the Atlantic's bottom. Strong winds have carried away boats and men, fires have consumed ships and crews, hulls have splintered and sails have split, causing vessels to crash against the shore and break apart. Even enemy submarines during World War II fell victim to the hazards of the Delaware Bay.

The Delaware Coast also has served as the repository of dead crew members and passengers. As the booty washed up on the shore, locals carried off possessions. In some cases, bands of heartless brigands stripped bloated bodies of their valuables.

By far the most famous story of the wrecks off Lewes is the disappearance of the British Sloop of War H.M.S. *DeBraak*, which sank at Cape Henlopen on May 25, 1798—200 years ago.

While conducting research for this book, I visited Hazel D. Brittingham, one of Sussex County's best-known writers and Lewes' premiere historian. Her files and records of local history are more organized and better equipped than many of the state's public libraries or newspaper morgues.

When talk turned to the *DeBraak*, she immediately provided me with volumes of information, including book references, numerous newspaper clippings and detailed magazine stories.

Following are only the highlights of the legendary ship's story.

The one-masted cutter *DeBraak* was built originally in England. Later, it was captured by the French during the American Revolution and, in 1781, it was sold to the Dutch. In 1795, the *DeBraak* was captured by the British and, in 1797, it was commissioned into the Royal Navy and placed under the command of Capt. James Drew.

While sailing as part of a convoy in the North Atlantic in March 1798, Drew was separated from the rest of the fleet in a storm. Two months later, on May 25, the *DeBraak* appeared at the mouth of the Delaware River. Accompanying Drew's ship was the *Don Francisco Xavier*, a Spanish merchant ship that Drew had captured earlier in April.

As the two ships dropped anchor, a sudden storm hit the area. The *Don Francisco Xavier* survived the harsh winds and waves, but the *DeBraak* heeled over, flooding her open gun hatches and taking on water.

Unable to right itself, the British ship sank to the bottom of the sea in a very short time. Drew, who was about to go ashore to Lewes in a longboat, was sucked beneath the surface to his death, along with 34 members of his 82-man crew.

Several days later, the captain's body washed up on shore, and he was buried in St. Peter's Episcopal Church Cemetery, located in the center of Lewes. Today, his captain's chest—which floated to the beach carrying three Spanish prisoners to the safety of the shore—is on display in the Zwaanendael Museum.

Many of the nearly 50 crew members who survived the sinking of the *DeBraak* swam for safety to the *Don Francisco Xavier*.

Since the DeBraak's masts could be seen above the surface at low tide, the British fleet sent salvage vessels to the site in September to try to raise the ship and pull her to shore. Eventually they gave up and left the area.

But, the fact that the British had shown immediate interest in the doomed ship reinforced rumors of treasure that had circulated since the disaster. Locals had been fascinated since many of the survivors claimed that the *DeBraak* had captured several Spanish treasure ships and the spoils were stored in the sunken ship's bowels. Other townsfolk verified that members of the crew had indeed paid for services and supplies with Spanish gold coins.

With the ship underwater off shore, with a few gold coins in evidence and with British salvage ships recently on the scene, stories of millions of dollars worth of treasure and gold took hold. As the years and centuries passed, the size of the *DeBraak's* fortune grew.

A sampling of newspaper headlines from local and regional newspapers tell the story of the periodic, but never ending, efforts made to locate the *DeBraak* and secure her riches.

DeBraak TREASURE
Dr. S. Pancoast's Great Undertaking at Lewes
Millions of Dollars' Worth of Gold and Silver
at the Bottom of Delaware Bay
—July 23, 1887

HUNTING FOR TREASURE
Divers Lose Track of the *DeBraak* Mound Off Lewes
—*The Morning News*, 1888

13

MORE FROM THE DeBraak
Additional Evidence of its Presence Discovered on Sunday
—*The Morning News*, Aug. 10, 1888

SALVAGERS IN LEWES BELIEVE SUCCESS NEAR
Boston, Fitted to Seek DeBraak Gold
Safe In Gale, Ready for Task
—Aug. 26, 1935

SALVAGERS 'PUNISH' DeBraak JINX EFFIGY IN SALTY WAY
—Nov. 15, 1935

DeBraak GOLD HUNT WILL BE RESUMED THIS MONTH
—July 13, 1936

EFFORTS GO ON TO SALVAGE DEBRAAK'S GOLDEN CARGO
—1936

Treasure hunts have involved companies, divers and experts from several states, some with extensive salvage experience. Other informal, local treasure hunters had combed the floor of the sea over the centuries, scooping up small numbers of artifacts, coins and, in some cases, human bones.

In the Oct. 26, 1985, issue of the *Delaware Coast Press* focusing on area ghost stories, writer Dave Hugg reported on the legendary claims by older residents who said they had "seen one of the area's most famed wrecked vessels—the DeBraak—under full sail in the Atlantic off Cape Henlopen. Others have claimed that, during a storm, they have seen the DeBraak 'sink, right before their eyes' in waters near where the old Henlopen Lighthouse once stood. A few have even claimed that they not only witnessed a reenactment of the May 1798 sinking of the DeBraak but have even heard the wailing of the drowning sailors and Spanish prisoners who lost their lives."

Don't Forget the 'Weather Witch'

One of the most persistent and fascinating legends related to the DeBraak and other unlucky ships that visited the Lewes area involves the "Weather Witch" or "Bad Weather Witch." Hazel D. Brittingham mentioned that this was one of her favorite local tales of the unexplained.

The celebrated witch of the Henlopen Cape is said to be responsible for churning up the waters of the bay to such a fierce degree that she has sunk ships and delayed salvage of the *DeBraak*.

Repeatedly, divers and ship captains have stopped treasure seeking operations because of long stretches of rain and wind, unexpected storms and bad luck—all caused, claim the locals, by the Bad Weather Witch. In November of 1935, after several weeks of rain and wind, Clayton Morrissey, captain of the salvage schooner *Liberty*, took serious action.

Morrissey gathered his crew and told them he was going to break the hex of the damned and cursed "Bad Weather Witch."

A newspaper at the time reported: ". . . he was ready to try the traditional 'jinx breaker' known as a cardboard effigy. It was a solemn ceremony in which all his seamen had implicit faith. They stood quietly in a group while the captain drew the picture of the jinx on a large piece of cardboard. The picture was a composite figure of all the evils known to seafarers. The next step was to 'punish the witch,' and each sailor, including the captain, took pot shots at the effigy, throwing such missiles at hand and riddling it with pistol shots. Then a match was touched to the witch when all stood around while the flames destroyed the effigy. After that, operations for the day were resumed."

Unfortunately, Charles Colstad, an engineer on the scene at the time, said that the only result was more interference from bad and nasty weather.

Some believe the "Bad Weather Witch" jinx dates back to 1799, when the British frigate *Resolute* tried to raise the *DeBraak* and was near success—until the lines snapped and further attempts were ended.

In 1932, a Baltimore firm tried to locate the site of the *DeBraak*, but the salvage boat *Katie Durm* caught fire, and it burned near the shore. In addition, that ship's sister craft, the *Cap*, was grounded while traveling through the Chesapeake and Delaware Canal, nearly drowning some of her crew.

In August 1986, when the *DeBraak's* fragile hull was finally scheduled to be raised to the surface, the "Bad Weather Witch" made her presence felt and affected the final sequence of discovery and salvage. A flat, calm, early morning sea changed to a windy scene shortly after sunrise. This weather condition and other mechanical malfunctions caused the salvage crew to abandon original plans that would have stabilized the remnants of the hull of the sunken, sand-covered craft.

As the DeBraak was raised—not in daylight, but in darkness, since it was close to midnight due to delays—artifacts were lost and sections of the fragile hull fell back to floor of the sandy sea.

So, even on the last day of the DeBraak's solitary life on the Lewes sea bottom, the "Bad Weather Witch" exercised her influence and mysterious power.

Today, more than 20,000 artifacts from the DeBraak are preserved. Among them are clothing, weapons, tools, personal items, wigs, foodstuffs, navigational objects, artillery, cannonballs, anchors, hardware and window panes. Some items rest in water tanks to protect them from deteriorating. Others are on display in Sussex County museums.

But, while it took 188 years to locate and raise the ship, all the mysteries associated with the famous 1798 shipwreck will never be over. Only a small portion of the millions of dollars of reported treasure from the DeBraak has been located and secured. And even fragments of human skeletons of lost crewmen have been hauled up with the artifacts.

"I was one of those who was disappointed when they brought a piece of it [DeBraak] up," said Hazel D. Brittingham. " I think mystery is more important than a mystery solved."

Many millions of dollars have been spent to find the DeBraak. The searches have involved individuals, small family enterprises and large corporations, several formed for the sole purpose of locating the sunken wealth—which had been estimated at many millions of dollars in gold, coin and jewels.

In the end, the amount of historic artifacts located far outnumbered pieces of eight, gold, emeralds and diamonds.

The locals in and around Lewes know more about the DeBraak than all of the sophisticated, high-tech, expert salvage hunters. They realize that much of the lost ship's structure, contents and story still remain buried at sea. In daylight and darkness, when the witch is resting and not on guard, area seafarers still head out from Lewes to scrape the floor of the sea, looking for more of the DeBraak's riches.

Others walk the shoreline immediately after a storm, looking for anything the "Bad Weather Witch" might toss up for strolling vacationers and serious scavengers along the Lewes sand.

Raising the Dead at Fort Delaware

W e raised the dead at Fort Delaware on Friday night, Aug. 29, 1997. It wasn't supposed to happen. It certainly wasn't a scheduled part of the 1997 Lantern Ghost Tours. But it's nothing that any of us who were involved are bothered by. After all, what better advertising for a ghost tour than having a few participants tell others that they actually saw an apparition?

But, I'm getting a little bit ahead of myself. Let me start at the beginning.

Pea Patch Island and the Fort

In the middle of the Delaware River, east of Delaware City between the opposite shorelines of Delaware and New Jersey, stands Pea Patch Island. According to legend, several hundred years ago a boat carrying peas and stones was grounded on a shoal in the middle of the river. Soon the cargo of peas sprouted, took root and formed the beginnings of the island that has since grown to its present size.

In the late 1700s, Major Pierre L'Enfant, who designed the layout of Washington, D.C., recommended that military fortifications be constructed on the island. It was during the War of 1812 that the first defenses were established, and others were built afterwards. The current fort, in the shape of a large pentagon, was completed in 1861. These fortifications, constructed of granite and brick, were built to protect growing cities along the Delaware River, particularly Philadelphia, Wilmington and the New Jersey coastal towns.

Its strategic location, armed with scores of cannons, made it a formidable defense against any enemy ships that might attempt to pass. Combined with Fort Mott in New Jersey and Fort DuPont on the Delaware side of the river, this three-station artillery defense provided excellent protection of the important shipping lanes leading to Philadelphia. This strategy continued until the period after World War I. However, these forts became obsolete with the construction of more sophisticated artillery defenses at Cape May, New Jersey, and in Delaware at Fort Miles at Cape Henlopen and Fort Salisbury near Milford.

As history has verified, no ships or enemy troops ever challenged the Fort Delaware defenses. Its cannons were never fired in anger. No battles were fought on its small patch of soil. But it did play a significant role in the Civil War, and today it stands as Delaware's only tangible link to the War Between the States.

Initially, no one thought of using Fort Delaware as a prison. But, in the earliest days of the Civil War, decision makers in the U.S. War Department decided that the fort's isolated island location was ideal for use as a prison.

In April 1862, 258 Confederate prisoners, many from Virginia, became the first of 33,000 Southern soldiers who would eventually be imprisoned on the Delaware River island. Since the fort was not built for use as a prison, the first captives were housed in rooms with little ventilation that had been built as powder magazines to hold ammunition.

These sites eventually became known as the "dungeons." But, as more defeated Rebels arrived, the inside of the fort was overflowing with prisoners, and new facilities were constructed in the marshy wetlands of the island. These wooden shanties provided little heat in the damp winters—the prisoners had one stove for every 200 men—and poor ventilation during the humid, mosquito-infested summers. Eventually, up to 13,000 Confederate prisoners were held captive at one time, during the summer of 1863—immediately following the Battle of Gettysburg.

At that time, historians believe that Fort Delaware was the largest populated city in the state of Delaware.

Death, however, also set up shop on Pea Patch Island. Poor living conditions and rampant disease are said to be the largest killers of the Rebel captives. Because the health conditions were so deplorable and contributed to the death of so many prisoners, some historians have referred to Fort Delaware as the "Andersonville of the North," in a reference to the infamous Georgia prison where many Yankee captives died from neglect and disease.

According to some records, approximately 2,700 prisoners died at Fort Delaware. Seven of those were shot, 11 drowned and the rest succumbed to the ravages of sickness and disease.

In a brochure provided to visitors at the fort, entitled *Prison Camp Trail*, Dr. W. Weir Mitchell, a Philadelphia surgeon who visited the fort in July 1863, when it was most crowded, described the conditions as "an inferno of detained Rebels."

Weir said, "A thousand ill; twelve thousand on an island which should hold four; the general level three feet below low water mark; twelve deaths a day from dysentery, and the living having more life on them than in them. Occasional lack of water and, thus, a Christian nation treats the captives of the sword."

Because of the high water table, the dead were not buried on Pea Patch Island. Instead, 2,436 deceased Confederate soldiers were transported to what is now known as Finn's Point National Cemetery in New Jersey. Their names are listed at the base of a tall monument, but they rest in unmarked graves.

Also in the brochure *Prison Camp Trail* there is a statement from the journal of Robert James Coffey, of Company G, 202nd Regiment, Pennsylvania Volunteers. The Yankee soldier wrote, "We took boats over to the New Jersey coast for burial, and sometimes five or six in one day. This . . . was a harder duty for a soldier to face than any fight upon the field or picket line. To have to jump into a boat with five or six men who died of smallpox or other deadly and contagious fevers was a bitter pill to swallow."

Other Rebels, deciding they had nothing to lose—tried to leave the island before they were sealed in a six-foot wooden box. An unknown number—perhaps more than a thousand— escaped or died trying to do so. Some hid in coffins or disguised themselves as Yankee guards. Others made rafts of driftwood, used canteens as floats or stole small boats. And, perhaps the most desperate, slipped through privy holes and swam toward the river and freedom.

In July 1862, more than 200 prisoners escaped the island in a single night. The aim of many of these Confederates was to reach the Delaware shore, hook up with some of the many Southern sympathizers in the First State and make it back through Maryland to Virginia. In later years, some Rebs would hope to escape and join up with C.S.A. Maj. Gen. Jubal Early, who, they had heard through smuggled news, was conducting raids against federal troops in nearby Maryland.

Who knows how many Johnny Rebs perished in the cold, swift flowing waters of the Delaware River while trying to reach shore? That is one question that will never be answered.

But some believe that many restless spirits, who were unable to return to the familiar soil of their Southern homeland, still roam the coastline of Delaware. On dark, misty nights, men in wet gray uniforms have been seen in the alleyways of Delaware City, along the waterfronts of the coastal towns of New Jersey, and in the reeds and brush of the Pea Patch Island wetlands. Frustrated, these unsettled specters appear lost and weary from years of seeking the eternal rest that they have never found.

The Tours

In April of 1997, Lee Jennings, park manager and historical interpreter at Fort DuPont and Fort Delaware came up with an idea—evening ghost tours of Fort Delaware—and he asked if I would be interested.

He said the concept was perfect. Lee and interpreter Dale Fetzer would do the history and I would do the horror. Jennings, an experienced re-enactor and historian is also the state park's naturalist and has been extensively involved in developing its acclaimed living history programs. He told me that he had been on tours offered at Williamsburg, Virginia; Charleston, South Carolina; and Gettysburg, Pennsylvania. All the other programs, he said, use one tour guide, who provides either history or ghost stories. Fort Delaware would be the only historic site that would present its program using several guides, and we would offer both historical and supernatural perspectives.

Having been to Gettysburg, I could understand his comments. While the battlefield is reported to be the premier haunted-ghost gathering site in the country, it has suffered dramatically from the intrusions of progress. Automobile traffic clogs its historic streets and roads cut directly through the park's hallowed battlefields. Commercialism creeps along beside the 19th-century structures, and the area is, essentially, the site of a new battle—where yesterday is fighting to hold back today.

On Pea Patch Island, Fort Delaware stands in magnificent isolation. No paved roads, no telephone poles, no shops, no telephones, no music intrude upon the historic prison. If you stand on the Delaware City dock in early morning and gaze east toward the granite walls in the distance, the scene is almost identical to that viewed from the watertown in 1861, at the start of the Civil War.

If ghosts had a choice to appear anywhere, what better place than Fort Delaware?

We agreed and Lee scheduled three programs, one each in June, July and August.

In the spring, before the annual arrival of regional daytrippers and school groups, we toured the Civil War-era fort. After a few sessions, we worked out the route of the ghost tour and planned our stories. Lee said he would even arrange to have a few state park personnel in costume, to add a bit of authenticity and eerieness to each ghost trip.

Each evening tour began on the Delaware City dock with a brief welcome and a short historical orientation of the island and important role that the fort played in the Civil War.

Just before the beginning of the premier tour, on the evening of Friday the 13th, Lee Jennings and I surveyed the waiting crowd. Not knowing what to expect, I saw a dozen Civil War re-enactors. The men were in full dress Confederate uniforms, and the women wore the hoop skirts, boots, caps and shawls of the period.

I thought to myself: *Lee really pulled in the big guns. These people will certainly add to the evening's authenticity and excitement.*

But, when I asked him about his cast of costumed participants, he told me he had no idea who they were. We soon learned that the group of re-enactors had decided on their own to show up in period clothing for the tour, and their presence was appreciated by the rest of the group.

One interesting thing we discovered were the stories. Not our stories, but tales shared by some of the passengers about their past experiences on the island. It was quite common for tourists to pull one of us aside and tell how they used to visit the island after it was abandoned by the federal government in 1944 and before it was taken over by state in 1948.

One gentleman, Bill Jenkins of Elsinboro, New Jersey, near

21

Salem, told me that many years ago, when he was 12 years old, he and a friend went over to the island, "blazed a trail through the tall grass, scaled the walls and went inside with a flashlight. It was eerie," he recalled, smiling, obviously proud he had a good tale to tell.

"We went back into the dungeons. It was pitch black. And we heard a 'clop, clop, clop' coming up behind. There was no way out. I could hear the sounds getting louder and then breathing, real close. We pictured in our minds that it was a Confederate prisoner with a peg leg. I took the flashlight and shined it straight in the direction of the sound . . . and it was a billy goat, with a goatee and horns staring right at us."

Laughing, he continued, "I swear, if it had a Confederate hat on I would have dropped dead on the spot. I found out they used to graze goats on the island for a while. Well, that's my story. You can share it if you want."

One of the Fort Delaware State Park staff who also presented the historical portion of the evening tours was Dale Fetzer. The nationally known historical interpreter has worked as a consultant on the historical films Andersonville and Gettysburg and is well respected in the field. Being a Civil War expert, Fetzer also was able to respond to questions about the Civil War unrelated to Fort Delaware.

Prior to one of the season's later tours, he related a story he was told about the "Headless Major." The tale goes that an old caretaker of the fort used to stop in at a local Delaware City ginmill after his shift. On one evening, he came in terrified and shaking. He said he saw a "Headless Major," dressed in a Confederate uniform roaming the ramparts.

Fetzer also shared another story that was to become a part of our repertoire as the summer progressed. Several years ago, a local artist spent a considerable amount of time on the island, painting wildlife scenes near the nature trails to the north of the fort.

After being there several months, she became familiar with the park personnel and got to know many of the staff on a first-name basis.

One afternoon she looked up from her sketch pad and noticed a young boy walking toward her. He was some distance away. As she continued to draw, the boy drew closer, near enough that she could make out his clothing—a red shirt, tan shorts, dark hair. She estimated that he was about 12 years old and saw that he was soaking wet, like he had just jumped out of a shower with his clothes on.

Looking down at her painting again, for no more than two seconds, she raised her head and the figure was gone. Thinking no more about the encounter, she completed her work and later took the boat back to the mainland.

As she passed by the office, she saw the park superintendent and mentioned her sighting, laughing at the time and adding that she was sure it wasn't a ghost because it wasn't wearing a Confederate uniform.

The man asked her what the boy was wearing, and she responded with a description of the soaked clothing.

Softly, the park superintendent replied, "That sounds like the boy who washed up on the island two days ago. He fell off a boat and drowned, and he was wearing a red shirt and tan shorts."

Thus, another ghost tale was added to the Fort Delaware lore.

As we mingled with the crowds before departure, we could tell from the informal conversations and brief comments that a large number of each boatload of tourists were hoping to "see a ghost." Many continued to discuss the possibility as they rode on the *Delafort* toward the Pea Patch Island dock.

During the summer of 1997, some would not be disappointed.

The general outline of the premier season's Lantern Tour included about seven stops, with stories told at each site. There also was an opportunity for questions and answers through the evening.

The first presentation took place in the shadows of the sally-port, immediately past the drawbridge entryway. This was followed by a visit to the Confederate officers' quarters in rooms directly above the fort's main black iron gate. Next, we stopped in the Polish Room where the series of tales of history and horror continued.

A discussion on hauntings took place in the fort's kitchen, and this was followed by a brisk walk—in rapidly disappearing sunlight—across the parade ground.

Saving the best until last, Jennings and Fetzer then led the single file of ghost hunters through the corridors of the "dungeons." This is where the lanterns came in handy. Damp walls, puddles of water on the uneven floor, deteriorating brick walls, minimal light and low-flying bats added to the atmosphere and charm.

A few claustrophobic guests had to be coaxed through the narrow passageways, but they found their effort worthwhile as they listened to tales of the extended solitary confinement of

C.S.A. Gen. James J. Archer, psychic tales related to the Lincoln family and hauntings by the Lady in Black.

A picturesque boatride back across the Delaware under a starlit sky and a few local ghost stories on the Delaware City dock completed the haunted outing.

Man in the Cloak

The sightings that many had hoped to experience began on the evening of the first tour—Friday the 13th of June. About two weeks later I received a letter from one of the Confederate re-enactors. The lady had taken a camera with her on the tour and had shot two rolls of film.

She had been accompanied by her brother and a number of friends. Some of the highlights of her letter follow:

"My brother is a Civil War re-enactor, and on several trips we have encountered energies at Fredricksburg, Va., and at Gettysburg, Pa. The film we had developed from the June 13th trip show five photos with unusual, unmistakable images or bursts of energy.

"One set of shots were taken just down from the kitchen. Here, along with several other re-enactors, I experienced a 'bad' feeling—one of fear. The shot shows strange energy curves and wisps.

"The second set of shots came from the long hall below the ground [dungeons]. Here I felt sadness, hopelessness and I kept thinking, 'My home, who are you?' as if we (the group) were intruding. The shots are warm, with unexplained glows. We were at the end of the tour here, and I felt we were being followed, always looking behind me. Several members of the Civil War group called prior to the films' development and reported these sensations."

When I spoke to Lee Jennings about the letter, he said the writer who had taken the photographs had brought them to the park office. "It looked like she had caught something with her camera during the tour," Lee agreed.

The other major encounter occurred on August 29th, during the next to the last summer trip.

After concluding my last story beneath the dock's flagpole in Delaware City, the crowd began to disperse. As the tourists were beginning to turn away, two of the park staff that had worked on the island that evening called the tour group back and asked for their attention.

The workers wanted to know if any of the passengers had been walking on the second-floor level of the casements, on the side of the island that faces New Jersey.

Apparently, several members of the tour group, and all of the staff who were standing beside each other at the time, did see a figure wearing a black cloak and carrying a lantern along the second-level restricted corridors. The workers said the sight was both eerie and unnerving, especially when they confirmed that all of that evening's staff were standing together. There was no way the mysterious figure could have been one of them.

The "Man in the Cloak" appeared again later, near the edge of the parade ground. But whatever it was disappeared before it could be approached.

"No one will get in trouble," the young worker told the group, "we just need to know if anyone from the tour happened to be up there with a flashlight or lantern."

Many shook their heads negatively in unison. I noticed that a few sported smiles, as if they thought the staff was putting on an act for the ticket holders' benefit. But, it was no ruse.

One of the young girls who had been working that night put her hands on either side of her mouth and whispered, "Oh, my God!" as she moved her head back. Apparently, she was shocked that the "Man in the Cloak" could be a real apparition.

No doubt, some of the passengers were delighted that they had been so very close to experiencing a fleeting wisp of the nether world. But for those of us who worked on the island that summer, this bizarre development was more satisfying than surprising.

Many, myself included, believe that an appropriate setting— that as close as possible duplicates historic conditions—is essential to entice the spirits to appear. Fort Delaware, isolated for more than a century on Pea Patch Island, does this better than most other historic sites.

In 1997, the psychic surface was scratched. In coming years, as the Ghost Lantern Tours continue, who knows what other restless specters may be awakened?

Why not join us and see if you're lucky enough to help raise the dead?

Historical notes: The state park, including Pea Patch Island and the fort, is under the jurisdiction of the Division of Parks and Recreation of the Delaware Department of Natural Resources and Environmental Control. Volunteer assistance is provided by the Fort Delaware Society.

The fort is located on the island in the Delaware River. Access is by boat, operated by the Delaware River and Bay Authority. The park office and departure dock is located in Delaware City, at the foot of Clinton Street, several miles south of New Castle, Delaware.

Fort Delaware is open weekends and holidays from the last weekend in April through September. From mid-June through Labor Day, the fort is also open on Wednesdays, Thursdays and Fridays. Admission to the fort is free. There is a charge for round-trip boat transportation. In 1997, shuttle service was added to and from Fort Mott State Park in New Jersey.

Features: Caution is recommended in certain sections of Fort Delaware. Be aware of signs alerting visitors to keep away from restricted and possibly hazardous areas. No child under the age of 15 is allowed in the fort unless accompanied by an adult. Children's groups inside the fort must be under the direct supervision of adults.

A gift shop sells Civil War souvenirs and a wide range of books about the history of Fort Delaware. A series of special events and a living history program operate throughout the summer season. Call the fort for specific details.

Sightings: In the rooms above the sallyport, in the Polish Room, in the officers' kitchen and in the casements or "dungeons." Also, along the trails north of the fort, on the grass covered ramparts, on the second level of the fort that faces New Jersey and in the corner office of the administration building that was occupied by the fort's commander.

Contact: For information about the Fort Delaware Society, call (302) 834-1630. To make reservations for the annual Ghost Lantern Tours (for ages 10 and above), group tours of the fort and for details about special events, call the park office at (302) 834-7941.

Visit to Finns Point

T his is not a ghost story, but to understand the ultimate impact of Fort Delaware on the prisoners and their captors, I believe this short section contains worthwhile information about the history and heritage of our region.

A two-lane road off New Jersey Route 49 heads west toward the Delaware River and Fort Mott. Entering the state park, one's attention is drawn to a series of well-preserved, concrete coastal fortifications standing at the river's edge. Tourists climb the metal stairs that lead to the ramparts and observation houses above. Standing there, looking out over the Delaware River, one views the same land and seascape that was seen by U.S. Army defenders during the Spanish-American War and World War I.

From Fort Mott, the east side of Fort Delaware is clearly visible. The ancient, granite pentagon stands close to the edge of the New Jersey side of Pea Patch Island.

Originally designed to defend the Delaware River in the post-Civil War era, construction of the Fort Mott coastal artillery defenses started in 1872. The initial phase, with two gun emplacements, was completed in 1876. The site was expanded in 1896 and the number of gun emplacements was increased.

When completed, the 10- and 12-inch guns at Fort Mott had an effective range of approximately eight miles. At the time, that was a longer range than any of the naval vessels that might have been involved in an attack. Two tall, iron control towers, still located on the state park grounds, were used to direct and adjust the shellfire upon the enemy.

Combined with the firepower at Fort Delaware on Pea Patch Island and from Fort DuPont, located just south of Delaware City, the three-fort defense of the Delaware River was considered formidable.

However, sometime after World War I, construction of more advanced defenses occurred at Fort Salisbury, near Milford, and at Fort Miles, near Cape Henlopen, both in Delaware, and at Cape May in New Jersey. These defense improvements made the three upriver sites obsolete as defense installations.

As time passed the federal government abandoned Fort Mott. In 1947, the state of New Jersey took it over and opened it to the public in 1951.

Finns Point National Cemetery is an extremely isolated plot of land, less than a half-dozen acres in size. It's well off the beaten track, with a narrow road leading to and from its iron-gated entrance. It seems like it was hidden intentionally, behind mounds topped by tall swaying marsh grass and a low, well-kept granite wall that encircles the irregular-shaped plot of hallowed ground.

I had heard often about the resting place of Fort Delaware's Confederate dead, but never made the pilgrimage. When I walked the cemetery grounds in late December, the sky was overcast, a storm was expected that evening. It was a good time to be alone in the graveyard.

At the north end stands an impressive monument, 85-feet tall and built of white Pennsylvania granite. It was erected in 1910 by the U.S. government to recognize the 2,436 Rebels who were buried in New Jersey's Yankee soil. The monument's granite tip points to the heavens, but the wide, multi-tiered base is anchored to the earth and surrounded by large, bronze plaques that bear the name and state of each dead Confederate.

The officers and enlisted men hail from such distant states as Texas, Alabama, Mississippi, Georgia, Virginia and the Carolinas. They seem out of place in this northern state, especially on a day when the blowing wind and gray skies intensify the cold. While they are remembered by name on the oversized markers, each's individual gravesite will never be found.

According to Alica Bjornson, Fort Mott historic preservation specialist, the names of the dead Confederate prisoners were burned into the top of each wooden coffins and a piece of leather was placed over the names for protection. However, the caskets were placed three layers deep in large graves, but no one recorded the exact placement of the boxes. Fort Delaware records maintained a list of the names of the Confederate dead, but not their exact location. Later, the burial documents were used as the basis for the bronze identification plaques that rest at the base of the monument.

At the opposite end of the cemetery are the Union dead. Those soldiers from the North who died at Fort Delaware while guarding their Southern enemies. The Union marker was erected in 1879, above where the 135 U. S. soldiers were buried. But only 105 names were available. These dead, too, are identified by a single, engraved, stone slab, now surrounded by a white-columned cupola.

In addition to another section with the graves of Fort Mott military personnel and families, 13 small, identical, round-topped stones mark the resting place of soldiers who are buried very far from their homeland. These are German prisoners of World War II who died while imprisoned at For Dix, New Jersey.

In life, the Yankees and the Rebels, the G.I.s and the Nazis fought on opposing sides. They hated each other; they tried to kill one another; they each fought bravely for their own sacred cause. Now, decades after their respective wars have been settled and, in some cases, forgotten, our country is no longer North against South, and the Germans are considered one of our strongest allies. And all of these old warriors rest within the walls of a tiny, out-of-the-way, country graveyard . . . together forever.

Contact: Fort Mott and Finns Point National Cemetery are located only six miles south of the Delaware Memorial Bridge, off New Jersey Route 49, near Salem, New Jersey. The park has an informative Welcome Center on the grounds. For information, call (609) 935-3218.

Overnight in the Logan Inn

Astoryteller friend once told me: "There are no accidents. All things happen for a reason." The longer I live, the more I find her comments to be true.

One morning in early October, I was heading to work. It's a short seven-minute drive, and sometimes I don't even turn on the car radio. This day, about halfway into my commute, I hit the button and started listening to *Phil Valentine's Morning Show* on WWDB-FM, Philly's premier talk radio station.

Picking up the conversation between host and caller in mid stream, I heard, "Down here in Delaware, the Rockwood Museum is haunted . . . ."

Naturally, that caught my attention, and I thought: *That's neat. I wrote about Rockwood's ghosts a few years ago in my book* Welcome Inn.

Through a series of quick phone calls from the station, the producer had located me and I was on the air that morning. Soon afterwards, arrangements were made for an overnight stay with WWDB staff in a haunted house.

Our spirited sleepover began on the evening of Oct. 30—Mischief Night and also my birthday—and extended into Halloween morning at the Logan Inn. The historic restaurant and lodging place is located in the center of New Hope, Pennsylvania, a quaint rivertown on the banks of the Delaware River.

The History

New Hope is associated with a number of important events in our nation's history. It is important to understand the town's significance during the Revolutionary War and its role as a link in America's early canal system to appreciate the area's legends and ghost stories.

Originally, the Borough of New Hope was part of the territory controlled by the Lenni-Lenape Indians. The area was secured by William Penn through a land grant from King Charles II. The Logan Inn is the oldest building in the town. Built around 1722 by John Wells, the town's founder, it was established as an inn in 1727. The building was originally known as The Ferry Tavern, and it is the longest continuously run inn in Bucks County and one of the five oldest establishments of its kind in the United States.

The impressive building stands at the corner of South Main and Ferry streets. The three-story, stone structure has been expanded by several additions, and it features an interesting wrap-around porch. One can easily imagine travelers in Colonial days sitting under the wooden overhang, awaiting the stagecoach or carriage that would transport them toward Philadelphia or Baltimore.

A popular nearby tourist site is Washington Crossing Historic Park. The 500-acre state park, located two miles south of New Hope, preserves the site where George Washington prepared his 2,400 troops for a surprise attack across the Delaware River against the British and Hessians at dawn on Dec. 26, 1776.

Prior to that battle, at the end of the same year in which American patriots had boldly signed the Declaration of Independence, General Washington and his men had seen their fair share of defeat. The American army had been driven out of New York and it had lost the Battle of Long Island in August. Afterwards, the Americans were defeated at the Battle of Fort Washington, and were forced to retreat across New Jersey. The defeated and low-spirited survivors arrived on the Pennsylvania side of the Delaware River in early December.

On the other hand, 1,400 German soldiers, under Colonel Gottlieb Rail, took over the village of Titusville, north of Trenton, and embarked upon a month-long drunken binge that included parades, wine, song and other popular amusements of the time. Laughing at the potential threat from Washington's "county clown," ragtag army in nearby Pennsylvania, Col. Rail participated with his troops in drunken orgies in celebration of Christmas.

That Yuletide season in America saw its first decorated evergreen trees, compliments of the Hessian mercenaries, many of whom were incapable of standing, let alone fighting, during that festive Christmas week.

Aware of the Germans' tendency to drink spirits heavily during Christmastime, Washington had his men commandeer as many different-sized boats as possible from the surrounding villages. At dawn on Dec. 26, the hungry, shoeless and coatless Colonial Army surprised the well-trained and well-equipped Hessians.

Busy playing a card game on Christmas night, Colonel Rail ignored a note of warning about the American attack. He was killed in the battle along with dozens of his men. More than 1,000 Germans were captured, and only two Americans lost their lives.

Some historians consider the Battle of Trenton one of the turning points of the Revolutionary War, for the Colonial victory renewed the Americans' fighting spirit. Today, a 110-foot-high observation post, named Bowman's Hill Tower that was built in 1930, is a popular tourist destination. This site marks the spot where American sentries watched enemy movement along the river in the days prior to Washington's surprise attack.

Beside the Logan Inn is a portion of the Delaware Division Canal, which opened in 1832. This manmade waterway system of locks enabled mule drawn barges to carry coal, grain, whiskey and manufactured goods along a route that extended from Bristol to Easton. New Hope's Lock #11 was the only point on the canal where four barges could pass at one time, making the village an important transportation site.

The Visit

I arrived at the Logan Inn at 10:30 p.m. on Mischief Night. The town was dead with very few walkers moving along its streets and alleyways. A few regulars were enjoying drinks at the bar in the inn's Tavern. Bartender Julie Johnson showed me around and answered some of my questions.

Ascending the stairway to the second floor, I noticed the large, floor-to-ceiling wedding portrait of the grandparents of Carl Lutz, former owner of the inn. The gentleman in the portrait, who unfortunately at some point has had his painted head smashed in, wears a lavender boutonniere and his wife has similarly-tinted hair. Some say the distinct smell of lavender lingers in certain rooms and the scent also has been noticed in other places throughout the inn.

On my way to my room, Number 14, I met a young man named Mike. He said he had been lodging at the inn for several months. A proud regular, it didn't take much urging to get him to share the strange stories he had heard.

"You've got to talk to the staff," Mike said, "but I will tell you that I heard that in Room 6 some people have seen the ghost of a little girl who drowned in the canal, right outside the inn. Also, during the Civil War, this place was a hospital, and a good number of patients died here."

Mike also recalled an incident that had occurred a few years ago. Two workers were repairing crumbling masonry on a stone wall beside the canal. While working, one of the men complained that he was being hit in the back of the head with stones, but when he turned no one was there. The annoyance continued throughout the day. Eventually, he noticed that the instigator was hitting him with pennies. Finally, he looked in time to see a small girl laughing at him, then she disappeared right before his eyes.

The pennies, by the way, were dated 1872.

Mike also mentioned the "Witch's Ball," a glass globe that sits on a special base behind the bar in the Tavern. He said he's been told that it's supposed to "trap evil spirits" that may enter into the building. It also has disappeared from time to time, but reappears in other rooms and on stairways in the building.

After thanking him for his on-the-scene report, I returned to the Tavern and was treated to a mini-tour of the old, stone-walled cellar by Julie the bartender. Leading me down the stairs, she said workers usually descend into the basement chamber cautiously and in twos. Rarely will a single worker go to the basement alone.

"Some say there are Revolutionary War soldiers buried down here," she said.

I mentioned I had been told that, during the Revolutionary War, some of Washington's troops died, but the ground was frozen so hard that they couldn't be buried. The lifeless bodies of the poor, waiting dead were stacked up like cordwood in the inn's cellar until the ground thawed enough to dig their graves.

She said that could be true, too. There were lots of stories about the inn, depending upon whom you asked. Pointing to a very large stone fireplace, she said someone even suggested that the decaying bodies were cooked and cremated in the walk-in-sized hearth.

"Once I saw a waiter come up from the basement. He got a chill down there and he really was white as a ghost. It's an old, rickety building, and you expect to hear things in a place like this. Almost anyone who has worked here for any length of time has been spooked in various ways. But if I ran into something, I'd be gone and never come back.

"In Room 6, its hard to control the temperature," Julie said, referring to the inn's most famous haunted room. "Sometimes, no matter what you do, it won't work right. It's our most popular room, and it's reserved well in advance."

A variety of specters have been associated with the building, including a Revolutionary War soldier who is said to stalk the halls. Also, a man in knee britches has been seen courteously bowing to guests before he politely takes his evaporated leave.

The most famous spectre is the little girl, who many believe drowned in the nearby canal. She has appeared in the inn's parking lot. There is a report that in the 1940s, while the annual street fair was being held in the inn's parking lot, it was interrupted because of the hysterical crying of a child. But police and fair personnel were unable to locate the sobbing child. The next year, when the howling cries returned, the fair was canceled for several years.

Early the next morning, before 4 o'clock, Al Egner, WWDB technician, was completing the mobile studio set-up in the Garden Dining Room. He was in charge of a vast array of wires, phone lines and portable speakers that were needed to communicate with the station and enable the show to operate on site.

Traffic wizard John Brown of the "Ghost" Patrol—renamed that one day in honor of Halloween—complained that his clock had been tampered with and his razor was missing.

Phil Valentine was at the microphone, speaking to his listening audience. Producer Ron Houston orchestrated the organized bedlam, maintaining contact with the station and instructing guests who arrived to share their comments and experiences.

During the period from 5 to 9 a.m., a number of listeners shared their experiences. One of the most interesting stories involved a man who worked in a North Philly bagel shop who continuously heard the strange sounds of someone pacing back and forth coming from inside the store's walk-in freezer.

A local musician was one of several visitors who stopped by the inn that morning. He explained that the entire region was rich in history. In fact, he said that in an old ferry home in Lambertville, New Jersey, there was a secret staircase that had been used by Benedict Arnold during the Revolutionary War.

"There was a lot of trauma and pain in the immediate area during that war," the New Hope resident said. "In my home, I've felt and seen a lot of things that I can't explain. Gigantic temperature changes, the radio turning on and off in one room, things missing. Sometimes the spirits show off."

Throughout the broadcast, Valentine, who spent the previous night in Haunted Room 6, mentioned his disappointment in not experiencing any ghostly activity.

I explained that we had spent about 12 hours in the Logan Inn, not enough time to become familiar enough with the site to notice anything unusual. The people who have worked there for years have more opportunities to experience the bizarre and are better able to notice something that might be out of the ordinary.

Traffic guru John Brown interjected that he considered the disappearance of his razor blade and the "messing up of his clock" proof enough that he had a ghostly experience.

As a result of Brown's repeated mention of his ghostly razor thief and unseen clock changer, Phil Valentine declared John Brown's overnight lodging site—Room 15—as the newest official haunted location in the inn.

The Ghosts

When investigating events that have occurred at haunted sites, the best results are found when four important characteristics are present:
- It is an historic site,
- It was the scene of a battle, personal conflict or serious trauma,
- Care is given to its historic preservation and
- The owners and management are proud to acknowledge the site's haunted presence.

Certainly, the Logan Inn complies with all of the above.

"This is an old building," Rorie Dean, wife of the inn's owner, said. "At the time of the American Revolution it was over 50 years old. There was a psychic here one year, when we were on CNBC. She said that 'absolutely' there was a headless soldier on the premises. They say the dead bodies of the soldiers were kept in the basement, and at least half of the staff won't go down there alone. There also are incidents and superstitions associated with the Indian weathervane of Chief Logan. Fires are reported to have started when the weathervane is disturbed. Now it's back on display and set up across the street."

Jeff Umbrell of Doylestown has worked in the Logan Inn for four years. He said a large number of people know of its reputation as one of the area's premier haunted sites.

"People often call and ask for reservations for the haunted room," he said. "We could get $500 a night at Halloween for Room 6. But for Halloween night it's usually rented about four months in advance. The local papers give it big play.

"When people ask, I tell them the well-known stories, like the bodies in the basement. One man asked if I would get him and his wife into the basement to look around. I told him 'No.' Then he said, 'What if I gave you a couple hundred bucks?' I still said no, but I felt like saying, 'When would you like to come?'

"In Room 6, some smell the presence of lavender. Others say there is a presence there, nothing to scare the daylights out of you. Some people have heard furniture moving around on the third floor. I met one woman who was a waitress at another restaurant," Jeff recalled, "and she told me she would never work here. But I like it."

Maggie Smith is the inn's manager. During her nine years at the Logan, she has experienced or heard of more than 50 minor and major unusual incidents. It's her impression, however, that most tend to occur on the second and third floors.

"There is a lot of noise in the closets in Room 6, both during the day and evening," she said. "I recall an incident during a weekday in February 1995. Two guests, a mother and daughter, came down and complained about a party that was going on all night on the third floor. They said it lasted until 2 or 3 o'clock in the morning. They were the only two people staying in the inn that evening."

Smith said a New York psychic who stayed in the inn said the headless soldier was not there to frighten anyone. "He just didn't realize it was time to go," she said.

In the formal dining room, a waiter named Michael said he heard a woman's voice call him by name. "He looked around and found no one,' Smith said. "He even looked out the windows. Then he came into the kitchen and was white as a ghost.

"The little girl story is that she sits or stands in Room 6 and watches. More psychics pick her up. They say she drowned in the canal. Some of the older stories refer to a man's crying face that appeared in a mirror in Room 6. There is a story about some people who left their shoes under the bed one night, and when they awoke the next morning all their laces were tied together.

"People are always calling, or we have them come in and ask about the ghost room. People come in just for that. Others want nothing to do with a ghost. But for most people it's fascinating. This is a wonderful building, and it's so old and exciting to be a part of. When people realize I work here, they say, 'Isn't that the place that has the ghost?' "

Adele Gamble, who has been operating ghost tours of New Hope for 14 years has stayed in the Logan Inn several times and investigated its hauntings.

"I think it is one of the greatest historic inns around," she said. "The ambiance when you go in is intense. You can just feel the energy. But, I must admit, I'm a little partial to it. There are so many ghosts in there, and you can feel so much history and so much energy, from the 1700s to the present. And I believe it will still be there after we're gone."

❊   ❊   ❊   ❊

Historical notes: The Logan Inn is the oldest building in New Hope. It was built around 1722 by John Wells, the town's founder, and originally known as The Ferry Tavern. In 1828, as part of the celebration of Washington's Birthday, the Ferry Tavern was renamed the Logan Inn, and a metal cutout of an Indian was put up towering above the inn's roof.

There are several stories about the origin of the metal shape of the Indian. One version suggests that the artwork was a tribute by the townsfolk to honor Chief Logan because the Lenni-Lenape was kind and hospitable to the white settlers. The metal Indian was a fixture above the inn for half a century and became New Hope's unofficial guardian or symbol of good luck. Today, it stands on a post across Ferry Street.

After closing for renovations in 1987, the historic inn reopened in 1988 with its original colonial charm restored. Antique woodwork, fireplaces and period furniture welcome a year-round flow of dining and overnight visitors. The Tavern reminds one of a stagecoach stop where travelers would gather for refreshment and conversation.

Since 1952, at nearby Washington Crossing, Pennsylvania, on Christmas afternoon re-enactors dressed in Colonial garb portray the events that took place in 1776. In 1997, approximately 250 re-enactors participated in the commemoration of the Delaware River crossing to the delight of an estimated 12,000 spectators.

Features: The Logan Inn offers 16 guests rooms, each with colonial period furniture, antiques and original art. All rooms have a private bath, air conditioner, color television and telephone. Deep set windows overlook the Delaware River and the main thoroughfare of historic New Hope.

Several murals in the bar were uncovered during renovations and carefully restored. Guests dine in the more formal Colonial Room or in the glass-enclosed Garden Dining Room, which features a stained glass wall. In season, dining also takes place on a large outdoor patio overlooking the main thoroughfare.

A private parking area, immediately behind the inn is a tremendous asset in the town with limited parking. Carriage rides through the town originate outside the Logan Inn. A walking ghost tour—where one can "Discover the Mystery and History of New Hope"—is a popular feature from June through November. For information, call Adele Gamble (215) 957-9988, who has been conducting the tours for 14 years.

Sightings: The scent of lavender manifests itself near the wedding portrait on the second floor. A Colonial soldier appears in the basement, and in the Tavern. Voices have been heard in the Colonial Dining Room. A man in knee britches has been seen on the basement stairway. A little girl ghost has been seen near the canal, in the inn's parking lot and in Room 6. This room on the second floor also has hosted a glowing presence and strange sounds have been reported in the closets. The movement of furniture has been heard on the third floor, and, in Room 15, John Brown's overnight rest stop, his razor blade disappeared.

Contact: The Logan Inn, Ten West Ferry Street, New Hope, Pa. 18938; telephone (215) 862-2300.

Illustration courtesy of the Logan Inn

Phantoms Near the Ferry

I didn't think this story was ever going to be printed. It began in the form of a letter sent by a friendly neighbor. I immediately knew it had potential, but I also realized that verifying the information was going to be difficult.

After completing a series of interviews over a two-year period, the disjointed, isolated facts from several interesting sources began to connect. As more details came to light, some of the incidents and comments that had been shared became understandable and the final story started to take shape.

The following chapter is the result of the thoughtfulness of the person who provided the initial leads, those who willingly shared their experiences and, it's probably safe to add, a dash of much needed luck that was provided by the unseen spirits who wanted their story told.

❋   ❋   ❋   ❋

I n January 1996, I received a letter from a neighbor containing the names and telephone numbers of two University of Delaware college students—Matt and Ben—"who had ghostly encounters during the summer while working at the ferry in Lewes, Delaware."

Matt and the Mysterious Mist

I met Matt in Jude's Diner in Newark, Delaware. It was winter, about 6 o'clock, and we shared a booth in the middle of the stainless steel tube that houses the short order restaurant. Our window overlooked Main Street. Since both the traffic outside and the business inside were slow, we had plenty of time to talk and no one nearby to overhear our conversation.

Matt admitted that he was eager to talk but, at the same time, a bit hesitant to share the unusual incidents that occurred during his summer job at the beach.

After the first cup of coffee and a few general, get-acquainted comments, the 20-year-old college student explained that he worked as a seasonal auxiliary traffic officer at the Cape May-Lewes Ferry Terminal in Lewes for the Delaware River and Bay Authority (DRBA). Essentially, he and others in the position served as backups to the regular, full-time officers. The summer workers directed traffic, took tickets, guarded the area at night and did whatever else was needed.

After three days of training, Matt, who is tall and thin with a crop of bushy, sandy-colored hair, was assigned to the midnight shift in the police administration building. The modern structure is located at the north edge of the parking lot, about a few hundred feet from the main terminal that is perched at the water's edge.

Matt laughed nervously as he recalled his first night alone on the job.

"It started happening right off the bat," he said, offering a weak smile. "The last boat leaves at 10 o'clock and, shortly afterwards, the rest of the shift was finishing up. One of the regulars stopped by the desk. As he was leaving he said, 'Have a good night and, by the way, did anyone tell you that the terminal building is haunted? And they say this whole place is built over an Indian burial ground!'

"He was with a ranger from Cape Henlopen. They both laughed and started working on me, teasing me about the burial ground business. Then, someone else added that a lady working in the gift shop had things jump off the counter once. As they left, someone shouted, 'Don't let the bogeyman get you!'

"I think it all kinda scared me. But I told myself that they were only trying to tease me, and I was falling for it. But I was feeling uneasy when everybody left."

After the cleaning crews were done, Matt was left all alone. He started his first set of rounds, drove throughout the complex, checked to see that all the doors were locked and headed back to the office.

"I figured if anything was going to get me it would have gotten me by then," he said, a smirk forming in the corners of his mouth.

All was quiet on the ferry compound until Matt completed his second tour of rounds. He arrived back in the office building at 2 a.m.

"I sat in the office for over an hour, watching TV and reading a book. I'd get up every now and then to walk around—trying to stay awake and not fall asleep. I was trying to be a good worker for the DRBA."

At 4 a.m., Matt was in the radio room, leaning back in a chair with his feet elevated, his heels resting on the edge of a metal desk.

Spreading a diagram of the office that he had drawn onto the diner table, Matt pointed out his exact position in the police building on that summer night.

He said that while glancing through an open doorway into the next room, he saw a black mist rising from the computer and copy machines, located about 10 feet away.

"It was a mist of black. Streams of it were going straight up, toward the ceiling, and I couldn't figure it out. I knew it was beyond my imagination. I decided that I should ignore it and it would go away."

It didn't.

"I got up and walked away from it, down the hall. Trying to let some time pass, I played solitaire on the computer. I remember that I wasn't scared, just uneasy. I was trying to not let my imagination get the best of me. I told myself: *Nothing will happen if I don't think about it.*"

About 10 minutes later, when Matt returned to the same chair the black mist was still rising.

"It was still coming out of the two machines," he recalled. "I sat there and stared. I kinda began to panic because, slowly, I started to see them kind of form into something like a shape of a figure. Then one of them started to move toward the room I was in. It was really faint, but it was there. I swear it!

"It looked like a human form, about 6 feet in height. It was like a shadow without being a shadow. I could see right through it. There was hardly any thickness or body to it. When it started walking, or floating really, I couldn't see any feet. It drifted into my radio room and I froze, just sat there perfectly still. I figured if it was going to hurt me it would have done so already.

"The strangest thing was that it came up to me and floated right through my legs. It stopped in the area of my knees and it felt cold. In fact, the entire room got considerably colder than it had been just a half hour before."

Matt said he raised his hand and put it right into the middle of the mysterious figure, but the black smoke went around his hand and through his fingers. His hand got very cold, too cold to keep it in the middle of the mist.

Other than moving his hand, he dared not move. While the mist intermingled with his legs, he stared directly at the specter, trying to memorize its features.

"There was no detail, as far as clothing or a face or structure," Matt said. "It had shoulders. It had arms. It had a definite head, but no legs. To me, it looked like a person without the legs."

Matt admitted that he had done a lot of thinking about the incident since the night it appeared. He pointed again at his diagram and said the figure stopped at the spot where the officers usually signed their daily report form.

"This may sound crazy," he said, "but I think he was trying to sign himself out for the end of his shift. I think it might have been a police officer who had passed away. It stood there for 10 or 15 minutes, maybe a little shorter. I wasn't watching the clock at that time, I was just trying to stay calm. Eventually, it left the area near my legs and the daily log and floated through the door. I looked at the clock then, and it said 4:40 a.m.

"I went outside to do my next rounds. I was just glad to get out of the building. I felt much safer outside."

Matt said he thought about leaving the ferry property and going to the nearest WaWa, but since it was his first night on the job he didn't want to get into trouble. A large part of him wanted to share his experience with someone else.

At 5 a.m. the morning crew started to arrive.

According to Matt, "One of the officers saw me and noticed I was pale. He said, 'Matt looks like he saw a ghost!' And I said, 'I did!' He had a good time laughing about that. He roared. I told him I saw a ghost, but I didn't share the whole story. If I did that, they'd think I was crazy.

"He said it was my imagination. Word got around real fast, and someone else said I was just alone all night and was imagining things. Then, somebody else shouted that if I wanted to have a good scare, I should go out to the monument near the water. It was erected for the people who died on the bay. He said on a quiet night, you can hear the ghosts screaming."

The entire morning shift had a good laugh at Matt's expense. When he returned the next evening, nothing happened.

42

"That was the end of the form," he said, looking at me across the diner table. "I never saw it again. But I did see smoke rising from computers, copy machines, filing cabinets, desks and tables. It didn't take any form, but floated up in streams toward the ceiling.

"I was there from the end of May to the end of August, about 90 days. I'd say the mist happened two or three times a week, at different times throughout the summer, always after midnight and only when I was alone. Every now and then I'd see a shadow pass by the doorway real fast. But the floating figure never came back to visit me.

"At first I was scared, but I realized whatever it was wasn't going to hurt me. It was just there minding its own business. I figured if I left it alone it wouldn't bother me. And I never told anyone else about the other things I saw. They'd think I was crazy. I got teased the whole summer for what little bit I said after that first night. I wasn't giving them any more material."

When I asked Matt if he every talked to the smoky mist, he nodded hesitantly.

"I'd try to make conversation with the streams of smoke," he said. "I'd say, 'Hi! My name's Matt. I'm stuck here overnight with you.' But I never got any response. Every night that it happened, I'd say, 'Hi! Don't hurt me.' By July, it didn't upset me at all. I just took it as part of working overnight."

Later, instead of telling anyone what happened to him, he made it a point to ask the old timers about any strange stories they knew about the area. As a result, Matt learned that he wasn't the only one who had witnessed unusual experiences at the ferry. He was told:

•A cleaning woman had been murdered in the area. Since she worked in the terminal building, she came back to roam the area,

•Cleaning crew personnel quit often because they would hear sounds and see toilet paper and towels floating through the bathrooms,

•Bathrooms that were cleaned and locked up at night were found to be messed up and dirty when reopened in the morning, and

•People standing on the ferry terminal patio near the water reported hearing voices moaning and screaming.

"On my last night working midnights," Matt said, "I was in a good mood, because I was happy to be getting out of there. But I will admit that a part of me wanted my ghost to scare somebody else. I thought it would be neat for him, or it, to scare the guys who were razzing me."

I wondered why the mysterious mist only materialized for Matt and apparently no one else.

He said he thought he had part of the answer. An officer told him that after a four-year break the midnight shift was reactivated the summer Matt joined the part-time force. Apparently, he was the first person to come back to work on the midnight shift since it had been discontinued.

"Maybe whatever it was had been waiting for company and I was the first one he saw," Matt suggested. "I don't know. To be honest, after all these years, I try not to think about it because it scares the pants off of me. I mean, not that many people have had an experience with a ghost."

So why did he agree to share his story with me, I wondered.

"I thought, well, it couldn't hurt. You're probably the only one who would actually believe me."

Ben and the Dark Shadow

I met Ben in Newark one afternoon. The University of Delaware student also worked as an auxiliary police officer at the Lewes-Cape May Ferry the same summer as Matt.

"I did ticketing and security," Ben said. "On the midnight shift, it was eerie. It was dark and there were all sorts of large hollow pipes. You could just imagine what was crawling around was in them. During the day it wasn't bad, but at night it was weird with the wind blowing. It was really creepy as you made your rounds. The wind sounded like a moan, and the chains were clanking on the flag pole. I guess being on the bay where it often was foggy added to the eeriness."

Ben thought he would find comfort and safety inside the police office radio room but, like Matt, he was unprepared for what he saw.

"It was during the midnight shift," he recalled. "I was alone and watching TV. There was a big window behind me. I had my back to it. I remember that the window glass was tinted, so it was hard to see outside. Even if you were outside and had your face right against the glass you couldn't see inside the building. About 2 o'clock in the morning, a human shadow formed on the wall behind the TV, in front of me, along the wall beyond where I was looking. It just passed right in front of me.

"It was like the sun was behind me and cast the shadow of an outline of a figure on the wall. It didn't move fast. It went fairly slow, and I sort of froze. I didn't think to get up and follow it. I just sat there for a minute. I was pretty concerned. After a few minutes, I picked up our computer log and went outside. I didn't want to be inside after that."

Ben said it took him about 20 minutes to settle down. His heart was pumping fast, and he had to concentrate on calming himself enough to go back inside.

"I don't know what I saw in there, but it was something. Then I started to think about the stories:

•The heavy doors that shut and no one was there,

•Things that fell off the counters in the snack bar,

•Hand dryers in the bathrooms that turned on by themselves and

•Hearing the cleaning crew over the intercom from the terminal building even after all the crew had signed out for the night.

"I had heard a lot of different stories from several people," Ben said. "I don't think the full-time people were trying to scare us. They said workers had seen a lot of stuff, but nobody had ever gotten hurt. Nothing had ever come after anybody."

Ben admitted he had spent more than a few idle moments trying to figure out what he saw. Each time he seems to come to the same conclusion: He isn't sure what it was, but he is sure what it wasn't.

"There's no way it could have been a shadow that was cast from the outside," he said, emphatically. "So whatever it was had to have passed in front of me. I told a few of the other workers and we even tested it the next day. To be honest, they weren't excited about it. Apparently, it was old hat to them. They told me they believed me, and they said it happened with some regularity.

"But I'm positive that I saw something unusual. And it wasn't my imagination and it wasn't because I was tired or falling asleep. We always tank up on coffee before we go on duty, because it's easy to doze off listening to the hum of the radio. I will tell you this, I was pretty much wide-eyed for the rest of the night. I wanted to make sure nothing got me."

The next evening when Ben arrived for duty, he got chills as he entered the building

"I was wondering if whatever it was would be back or if I would see something worse. I told a few of the other part-time guys and they were a little freaked because some of them had stories, too. And somebody mentioned that it might be the ghost of an officer who haunted the place."

Karen and the Lollipops

Karen has been working for the DRBA for a good number of years. Stating the exact number might give her identity away, so we'll just say she's been there long enough to see workers come and go—and she's heard a lot of unusual stories associated with the ferry.

"Things are so busy around the terminal during the day in the summer that even if a ghost floated through the room you might not notice it," she said, laughing. "But late at night, when things calm down a bit, it's a bit more quiet and easier to notice unusual things that might happen."

Like what?

Like the night she was standing in the closed gift shop and a tree-like stand filled with 50 lollipops "jumped" off the shelf and tossed the contents onto the floor.

"There was no one near it," Karen said. "It actually looked like someone pushed them out from the bottom. The police officer who was standing nearby couldn't figure it out and neither could I. I remember getting a real chilly feeling right then."

Karen said that one winter, while the cleaning crew was scrubbing sinks in the restrooms, the hand dryers went on by themselves. They are the type that must be activated by applying pressure against the silver button. But no one was there to press them into operation.

A visit by electricians the following day determined that the units were fine, the building circuits were in order and the power lines to the bathrooms were in perfect condition. "They told us there is no way they could have turned on by themselves," Karen said.

"One of the cleaning crew supervisors was complaining to us that she had a hard time keeping a crew and no one would tell her why. They would seem fine at night but call and quit the next day."

Later the boss found out that the ferry terminal's late shift cleaning crew was not comforted when the stations on the radio seemed to change by themselves, when doors opened and closed on their own, when the large metal refrigerator door latched and unlatched at will and when mysterious voices were heard calling some of the workers by name.

"In one instance," Karen said, "one of the cleaning crew was working from midnight to 4 a.m. in the bathroom and a misty white form came up out of the drain in the sink.

"There were other things that happened over in the police building," she added. "Some of the kids who worked there in the summer would come to see me saying they heard someone calling out, but they couldn't make out what the voices were saying."

Karen said the older workers usually keep the stories to themselves, until a newcomer brings up or asks about a strange or unusual incident.

"We don't want to scare them to death or they won't want to work here," she said, laughing. "But, like I said, it's a zoo in the summer. But in the winter it's so quiet that you have the time to pay attention—especially in January and February. There's hardly anybody around. It's scary at night, with the wind blowing off the water. One officer was on duty and thought he saw someone in the terminal. He went in to check. When he was ready to come out, he heard a weird sound. He said it was like the creaking of an old ship. He came out quick. Maybe it was the wind. Who knows? But little things go on from time to time. Equipment turns on and off on its own. Computers don't respond properly.

"Sometimes the night crew is really jumpy, nervous. A lot of people may experience things but not say anything. We have some officers who have passed away, and we try to take their names and numbers out of the computer system and they keep coming back."

Evelyn and the Hand

The graveyard shift was Evelyn's domain, working in the ferry's main terminal building after hours, cleaning restrooms and public areas when everyone else was gone.

"I used to live in a haunted house," she said, "so it didn't bother me when the hand dryers would come on by themselves. I took my radio in there, to listen to it by myself, and the volume would turn up and down and the channel would change with no explanation.

"Ice would come outta the soda machine in the middle of the night. And there was no one there to turn it on, and there was no cup to catch the ice—with no explanation. I seen puffs of smoke come outta the sink in the bathroom. White clouds. It never turned into a figure, but it was large white clouds."

Evelyn said she tried to determine a sensible explanation for as many of the strange incidents as possible.

"I said an electrical shortage caused the dryers, and I figured it was a gas buildup that made the puffs of smoke. But I couldn't find any logical reason for the large metal, walk-in refrigerator doors opening and closing or for the voices that were causing the mumbling sounds. Those I couldn't determine."

Evelyn said that most of the events she experienced were annoying rather than frightening. But there was one incident she'll never forget because it was more serious than all the rest.

"I was in the men's room," she said, "cleaning the handicapped stall door when I felt a full hand rest on my right shoulder. It was there long enough for me to feel it and I could feel that each of the fingers were there touching me, all extended. I turned and there was nothing, and there was absolutely no explanation for that one. I admit I was scared. I figured if I ignored it, I'd face no more abnormalities in there. But of all the things that happened, that is the one I will never forget. I left real quick that night."

Hazel and the Answer

Those four sources provided an interesting list of unusual events that occurred on the Delaware grounds of the ferry. But every good, true ghost story should provide a reason explaining why such a large number of bizarre things happened at a specific site—otherwise the reader is left with a litany of scary incidents but no satisfying conclusion.

In historical areas, the events often occur at the site of a battlefield where restless souls still roam. In an old inn or restaurant, a murder or sudden accidental death may have happened in the building.

To complete this Lewes ferry terminal ghost story properly the final puzzle piece that provided a possible explanation for the strange events was needed. The key, that would link all of the unusual incidents, was out there somewhere. It just had to be found.

The solution was provided during an unrelated interview with Hazel D. Brittingham, a well-known Sussex County historian and author. She had invited me to her Lewes home to discuss the

"Bad Weather Witch," one of her area favorite legends. (See story in this book entitled "Lewes: Delaware's Most Haunted Town?")

In the midst of our discussion, I shared my reports about possible ghosts in the area of the ferry terminal. When I mentioned my search, Hazel immediately headed for her filing cabinet and produced a file that held the key to the mystery.

According to a number of newspaper articles and other documents, the terminal parking lot was built over the "Unknown Sailors' Cemetery," one of the oldest public burial places in the state. In the early 1960s, some townspeople opposed the proposed ferry terminal road that would link the ferry dock with the Delaware mainland.

The following articles provided the details needed to answer the questions.

Lewes Ferry
Fight on Graveyard Has 1600s Precedent

"Opponents of the proposed Lewes ferry terminal road may find a solution to their problems and support for their cause by delving into historic records concerning another old cemetery. . . .

"Some believe the Unknown Sailors Cemetery, approximately 171 feet east of Lewes Coast Guard Station on the Delaware Bay shore contained some 800 graves.

"The presence of the cemetery was disclosed in 1939 with the finding of human bones disinterred by heavy seas against the shore. Old-timers believe there may have been small wooden markers but these were gone.

"One Lewes Coast Guardman, Capt. William Carson, then in his 80s, recalled the spot was a sailors' burial ground. . . . "

—Virginia Cullen, *Morning News*,
Wilmington, Sept. 14, 1963

Unknown Sailors' Cemetery
Salutes Men Who Gave Their Lives

"The ship made it inside the breakwater just before the worst of the storm hit. Through the snow, the shore was barely visible. The blizzard was one of the worst in memory; by daybreak, almost 100 ships had found refuge in the Delaware Bay off the shore of Lewes.

"But even the safety of the breakwater was not enough to save the lives of countless sailors who had been swept overboard, frozen in the rigging or drowned in the icy water after their ship had gone down.

"Now, nearly after a century, the resting place of the these hundreds of sailors who lost their lives will be permanently marked. [Through] The combined efforts of the Lewes Historical Society and the Colonel David Hall Chapter of the Daughters of the American Revolution, the Delaware River and Bay Authority will officially mark the burial site for over 500 unknown seamen.

"The site of the graves is east of the Cape May-Lewes ferry terminal where the parking lot of the facility is located.

"According to Henry Marshall, a Lewes historian who was instrumental in the movement to mark the spot, bodies of sailors would wash up on the beach where they would later be found by patrolling Coast Guardsmen or townspeople during the late 1800s. With no way to identify the sailors or preserve their bodies, the guardsmen were forced to bury the bodies just above the high water mark on the beach. . . . ."

" 'Many times they would bury the bodies right there on the spot,' said Marshall. . . . . "The blizzard of 1888 was particularly violent and one that cost the lives of many. 'The harbor was full of ships and some of the men froze right in the rigging.' "

—David Small, *Delaware Coast Press*
Lewes, March 16, 1983

Unknown Sailors' Cemetery in Lewes
To Be Dedicated in May 27 Service

"The Unknown Sailors' Cemetery, unmarked since the turn of the century, will receive recognition long denied it at 1:30 p.m., Friday, May 27, with a Memorial Service and dedication of a plaque.

"Located on the grounds now occupied by the Cape May-Lewes Ferry Terminal on Lewes Beach, the cemetery is the last resting place of an estimated 500 to 800 seamen, sometimes with their families, washed ashore in the age of sail. . . .

"The occasion marks the successful culmination of efforts undertaken over the years since the cemetery fell into disuse with the coming of age of steam. Efforts in 1939, when high seas disinterred some human remains, and again in the 1960s, when the ferry terminal was built, met with no success."

—*The Whale*, May 25, 1983

Cemetery at Lewes, Delaware

"Levi Lynch, another U.S. Coast Guardsman, also now retired stated that he recalls the cemetery and his recollections are very clear that there are many bodies buried east of the Coast Guard Station, for a distance of 400 or more feet, that the many buried were unknown sailors employed on merchant sailing vessels. Both he and Mr. Carson remember the main cemetery had a fence around it and that there were wooden markers, painted white with black letters, placed on some of the graves; these have long since disappeared, as has the fence that enclosed the main cemetery.

"It has been reported by some that there are at least four or five hundred bodies buried in this area, while others have placed the number between seven and eight hundred."

—Excerpt from a copy of the background
associated with Senate Bill No. 320,
passed by the Delaware legislature in 1939

Unknown Sailors' Cemetery Dedicated

"The project to mark the former cemetery on the grounds of the Lewes-Cape May Ferry Terminal came to a successful conclusion on May 21. Those buried there were memorialized and a plaque unveiled in an afternoon cemetery . . . .

"Mrs. Hazel Brittingham, member of the Lewes Historical Society Board and of the Cemetery Committee, unveiled the plaque which was made possible by the River and Bay Authority.

"The plaque reads:

Unknown Sailors' Cemetery

*Lewes has been a port-of-call and
a Harbor-of-Refuge since the 17th century.
For generations during the age of sail,
a public burying ground
in this immediate locality
became the final resting place for hundreds of sailors
who lost their lives and whose unidentified bodies
were here cast ashore.
In remembrance of those persons
whose remains are sheltered on this shore,
this memorial is placed.
May they find eternal repose.*

—Lewes Historical Society
Newsletter, 1983

So the mystery is solved, and a link with the bizarre has been discovered. Haphazard burials that took place over several centuries on the land at the ferry terminal area might be a possible explanation for the strange events that have been reported in the ferry's gift shop, restrooms and police building.

Soon after the source of the aggravation was discovered, I called the two students and told them about the old sailors' burial site. In both cases, the young men were not surprised. Instead, they were relieved that there was some kind of a reasonable explanation for what they still swear they saw.

The two young men both spent the summer working and walking over an estimated 800 unidentified restless souls whose bodies still lie beneath the ferry's blacktopped parking lot.

That being the case, one cannot ignore the unique possibilities that exist for some long-gone, determined sailor's spirited intrusion into the modern world. Imagine that on a warm summer evening, immediately after a storm similar to one that had deposited dead seamen in the sandy ground, the spirits awaken.

Maybe it's because of the thunder and lightning, or the loud sounds of the crashing waves and surf. The reason isn't as important as what could happen.

Suppose a few of these restless souls literally rise up and drift through the blacktop. Missing their usual entree into the present day—through the portal of the police building's copier and fax machines—they seep invisibly into empty, parked tourist vehicles. When the owners return from a visit to the snack bar, gift shop or restrooms they drive their vehicle onto the *Twin Capes*, the pride of the ferry fleet, and head across the bay into the Garden State.

And that restless, misty black cargo—lonely from so many long years under the sand—may be eager to show itself off in its new home, at the unsuspecting driver's residence.

Other Residents

I'm very thankful for the information I receive in the mail, as well as for the items that friends drop off at the house or stuff in my mailbox at work. Often, I'm not able to use the article or lead right away, but it's saved for a later time when it complements other material or details I've picked up in interviews.

About two years ago, I was given a copy of the West Chester, Pennsylvania, *Daily Local News*. The bold headline from the "Homes" section immediately caught my eye:

4 Bedrms, 2 baths, 1 ghost:
A real estate nightmare
Selling a home with skeletons in the closet can be scary

The wire service story, which was supplemented by a few local comments, consumed most of the section's first page, It included stories about several sites where the presence of invisible residents—ghosts—played a significant role in the sale and transfer of real estate. Interspersed throughout the printed columns were graphics of floating, balloon-like ghosts with wavy eyes and wide open mouths. The date of the paper was Oct. 18, 1995. This was one of the Halloween stories that newspapers carry every year to satisfy the seasonal needs of their readers.

The article told of a New York home overlooking the Hudson River that was haunted by the presence of several Revolutionary War-era ghosts. Even though they had not experienced any incidents, the potential buyers heard stories about the hauntings and decided to take back their deposit on the $650,000, 18-room, gabled mansion.

A state judge, the story continued, eventually declared the home haunted "as a matter of law," and the structure eventually sold for a much lower price.

Just the rumor that a home has been haunted—or was the site of a sensational, publicized crime involving torture or murder—can cause the selling price to take a dive. At times, it can even cause potential buyers to stay away completely.

In Hopkinton, Rhode Island, the remains of a person missing for 10 years were discovered in a home's septic tank. The current owner, who has lived in the home for a year, noticed a strange smell as he passed by a section of his back yard. Curious, he pushed back the concrete lid of the septic system and saw a human skull staring back at him. After the national publicity this tale generated, one can only imagine the additional charges the local honeydippers will lay on this unlucky homeowner when he calls to get his septic system cleaned.

Ever since we started the *Spirits Between the Bays* series, it was obvious that most people do not want the address of their haunted residence listed in the book or even shared in casual conversation. Whether to specify the location of the haunted site and use the actual names of the individuals involved are the first two issues that are discussed at the beginning of every interview we conduct.

In the overwhelming majority of cases, residents of private homes do not want any publicity. But, when we talk to innkeepers, restaurant owners and museum directors, most of them definitely want their site mentioned—along with their phone number, directions and hours of operation.

People love to visit haunted places. Entrepreneurs know having a resident haunt is good for their business and many museum operators are always looking for new ways to increase attendance. In some cases, a few friendly phantoms can give attendance a boost.

The *Daily Local News* article also noted that local real estate professionals find homes located next to cemeteries tough to sell.

If that's the case, imagine finding out that your secluded, high-priced, waterfront residence is built on an Indian burial ground, or that your brand new development home—sporting all the modern conveniences—is on top of the family plot that once stood beside the subdivision's original farmhouse.

While some believe it's best that anything unusual or paranormal about a home be told to serious buyers before a contract is signed, some think that such information may queer the deal or cause potential buyers to think the sellers may be a bit strange. Most experts agree, however, that it's better to be safe early in the game than sorry at the settlement table.

Following are a few stories I've been told about haunted sites in the area. I can give you the facts and the general location, but I cannot give you the exact address. Knowing they are out there may be of some help, but it's best to follow the age-old advice: Let the buyer (or renter) beware.

•A friendly and artistic couple I've known for the last 10 years lived in a beautiful Civil War-era mansion on the banks of a narrow Eastern Shore river, south of the Chesapeake and Delaware Canal. Their property was the home of a former sea captain. It was capped with a widow's walk, and there were several outbuildings, two stone ice houses and lots of rolling acreage. My friends said they spent more than 15 years restoring the home to its former grandeur. For more than 20 years, the family lived in the historic mansion, which visiting psychics and shamans agreed was "infested with ghosts."

As soon as they put the beautifully restored property on the market, they had a fair share of serious lookers. After a few months, the frustrated wife called me and said, "Everyone who comes to take a look simply loves the house. But, I don't understand it, the minute I tell them about the other residents they look at me strangely and then they never come back."

Apparently, in this case, telling the whole truth and nothing but the truth wasn't the best policy.

•In Kent County, Delaware, an old farmhouse near the Maryland border was used as an Underground Railroad stopping point for runaway slaves seeking their freedom in the north. They would paddle up river in small canoes, head into the marshland and, at night, make their way with the help of guides into the secluded outbuilding behind the main farmhouse and close to the marsh.

In the parlor of the plantation's main house there were two very large oil paintings. They extended almost from the top of the wall, near the ceiling, to the area where the wall met the floor.

55

The owner had installed special hinges behind the frames so he could hide slaves inside the special indentations he had built in the wall. However, he decided that it would be best if he keep the existence of the secret hideaways to himself and told no one else about them, including his wife.

Late one night, when the lady of the manor was away and the servants were asleep, he went out to the shed and led two families of slaves into his home. Carefully, he directed them to the special hiding places inside the walls, told them to keep quiet and not make a sound. Then he shut them behind the large paintings, where they were to wait until the next afternoon, when he would lead them to the next hideaway station on their journey.

Unfortunately, before morning the plantation owner died, and with him went the secret of the escaping slaves.

Legend says that the terrified slave families never called out, for they did not know if the persons on the other side of their hideaway would be friendly and helpful or evil and send them back to their former masters. They waited behind the paintings, in their secret spots, until they all died. Many years later, the passages were discovered and piles of dust-covered bones rested on the floor.

The current owners are careful not to tell the story to too many people. But, they swear that the tormented spirits still roam the house with abandon, seeking to take revenge on the man and his family who left them there to die.

•On the Eastern Shore of Maryland, an unmarried woman gave birth to a stillborn child. Embarrassed and afraid of the consequences, she tried to keep the baby's existence a secret from everyone. One night, when her family was asleep, she took the tiny body, wrapped it in a white cloth and carried it outside. Dragging a small shovel, she crawled under the house and buried the child in shallow ground in the back corner of the front porch. No one ever knew of her pregnancy, and no one discovered the tiny corpse that rested all those years directly beneath the rocking chairs that sat near the front doorway of the house.

Nearly 80 years later, new homeowners decided to tear out the old wooden porch and put in a modern one made of brick and concrete. When the young husband and wife pulled away the planks that formed the porch floor, they looked down and saw a wooden cross that had served as the tiny grave marker left by the sad young mother. As they dug a few inches below the surface, they discovered a small container, about the size of a cigar box. Inside was a note saying, "I am so terribly sorry. My God, please forgive me. Rest in Peace." Under the note, and in the frail white cloth, were the tiny, fragile bones of a stillborn infant that had been laid to rest.

Sitting on the new front porch, the present owners stressed that they love their home, and they've had no unusual experiences or spirited problems. They discovered what happened after piecing together some tales and stories from an old cleaning lady who used to work for the previous owners for many years. That old woman has since died, they said.

The young couple swore that I'm the only person with whom they've shared their strange story. And, they added, if they ever decide to sell their home, they would never tell anyone else about the baby's grave hidden under the front porch, especially potential buyers.

•Elizabeth and her husband have lived in their Delaware City house for 25 years. The home that's listed on the National Historic Register has never hosted any major unusual incidents, until recently.

The 150-year-old frame home was built before the Civil War. Periodically, Elizabeth said, they had experienced sounds that occur in all old houses—sudden noises that are mistaken for footsteps or the sounds of doors opening and closing. Usually, there's no apparent cause, except sometimes certain doors do seem to open or close on their own.

"At least the doors seemed to be open after we closed them, and sometimes it seems like they will shut on their own," Elizabeth said. "But one night my husband was away and I heard a noise that seemed to be coming from the first floor. I went down the steps to investigate, and there was a large, curly-haired, gray-headed man in the living room. I tried to remain calm and, to be honest, that wasn't hard to do. You see, he had a calming effect on me. I wasn't scared, I was more curious, actually."

Soon after her one and only sighting, Elizabeth shared the experience with her next door neighbor, an elderly woman who had lived in town for a very long time. When Elizabeth described her mysterious, early morning visitor, her neighbor said the phantom's clothing and physical size seemed to match Mr. Chippes— the former owner of Elizabeth's home. The man had lived there for more than 60 years.

"That was the only time I saw him," Elizabeth said, "and I've never been afraid. But we've had other things happen here. Clocks stop and start for no reason. Sometimes our stereo speaker is moved from its proper place, but it weights nearly 60 pounds, so that's not an easy thing to do. You see something like a shadow pass by, out of the corner of your eye, but when you look there's nothing there.

"I'm not afraid," Elizabeth said, smiling, "but since I've started sharing the stories about our place my teenage son doesn't want to stay home alone."

• Marianna and her daughter lived on the second floor of an old private home that had been turned into an apartment house in Pocomoke City, Maryland. It wasn't too far from the old white bridge that crosses the river in the center of town. After their first week in their new home, strange things began to happen.

"I was watching television with Rachel, she's my daughter," Marianna said, "when I saw a fat, gray snake, all curled up under the television. It was big and thick. I right away called up the manager, and he said he'd be right on over. But when I put down the phone and looked back, that snake, he was gone."

The manager checked all over the apartment, but the snake was nowhere to be found. Bothered by the sighting, Marianna left the apartment and stayed for a few nights with her sister in Princess Anne. Three days later, she and Rachel returned to their apartment.

"But that was the night of the rat," Marianna said. "I just shut off the television, and I saw this large mother of a rat. It came after me, chasing me down the hallway. Then it got me backed up into a corner and it just sat there, snarlin' and glarin'. It was horrible, and while I was screamin' for Rachel to help, the damned rat just up and disappeared. Just like what happened with that snake!"

That night Marianna and Rachel stayed in the same room and swore they were going to move out the very next day.

"It was like the minute I said that to myself," Marianna explained, "strange things started to happen in my closet. It was a

big one, a walk in. There was sounds comin' from in there like
something was throwing stuff around. Boxes were bouncin' off the
walls, and there was lots of bangin' and kickin'. It was horrible.
Kept us up all night long."

In the manager's office, Marianna threatened to tell everybody
the place was haunted if she didn't get her security deposit back.
The manager agreed, and then he shared a story with Marianna,
so she didn't think it was all her imagination.

"He told me that two brothers owned our buildin'," Marianna
said. "The one guy, he owned all kinds of boats and sailed all over
the bay. He used to have the place I was in fixed up special just
for him, so he could show off his ship models and sea collection.
Nobody else ever lived in there—except him and then me after.
But he just died only a few weeks before I moved in. So, I guess
he don't want nobody else in his private space. That's the way I
see it, and, to tell you the truth, I can sorta understand that," she
added with a smile and a shrug. "But I just wish he woulda said
somethin' before I moved in.

"I was outta there that afternoon," she added. "Lived back
with my sister for a few weeks, then got a new place. But I ran into
the manager a while later, an' he told me he tried to rent that
same apartment two more times, but nobody lasted more than a
week or two, each time. It's empty now, only used for storage, he
says. He still can't rent it to nobody."

•Donna and Bob are proud of their restored Victorian home.
Located on one the busiest streets in the heart of Lewes,
Delaware, the 120-year-old structure had experienced years of
splendor as well as several decades of neglect. In addition to serving as a home for large well-to-do families, it had been a boarding
house and, for a time, was rented out to several different tenants.

It's been 18 years since the retired couple moved into their
present home, and they laughed about how they also have adjust-
ed to the comings and goings of their resident ghost.

"We started thinking there was something strange about the
place soon after we moved in," Donna said.

"It was the dimes," Robert added, nodding his head as he
tossed out the comment.

The what?

"Dimes!" he said more emphatically.

Picking up on the story, Donna explained that soon after they began restoring the structure, the couple began finding dimes on the floor. The coins always appeared in a specific bedroom or in the hallway, directly outside the one doorway on the second floor.

"They weren't old coins," she said. "The dates were relatively recent, but they seemed to show up from time to time in the area near the bed."

At first, Donna said, she thought Bob might have had a hole in his pocket and the money was falling out. But that wasn't the case. "And I never took my purse that far into the house," she said. "The farthest it ever got was into the second-floor kitchen," she stressed. This and Bob's well-sealed pockets were proof that neither of the home's two mortal residents were responsible for the mysterious appearance of the coins.

Over a six-year period they discovered about 13 dimes.

On one occasion they lost a part to their vacuum cleaner. "We said the ghosts must have it," Donna recalled, "and Bob said they must be paying us rent for it. Obviously, we got to the point where we could joke about it. The interesting thing," she added, "was that the dimes always appeared in that one room or hall. Why didn't they appear in other parts of the house? I find that strange."

When they first moved into the home, a neighbor stopped by and wished them well but, Donna said, "She also told us we do have ghosts.

"But that news didn't bother me. I like them; and, I admit, I'm very sensitive to their presence. I will say this, if we have any, they are very friendly. I've been in houses where I've sensed an evil presence when I walked in the door. Once, when my daughter was looking for a place to live, we went into the cellar and I got a bad chill. It was so bad that the hair stood up on the back of my neck. I told her, 'You're not living here!' and we left."

Bob added that they also have heard voices in their home. It was the sound of several people speaking at the same time. Not a wild party, he said, but the sound of a group involved in an enjoyable conversation.

"We would wake up and hear it," Donna said. "I'd get up and go to the top of the stairs and try to make out what they were saying. It was like you felt if you could get just a little bit closer you would be able to hear the words clearly. But, just as you were almost close enough, the voices stopped. We were never able to pick things up."

Donna and Bob said they haven't had any activity recently. Maybe, she suggested, the ghosts are happy with the renovation. They've spent a lot of time restoring the home to its original beauty.

"I think that must be it," Donna said. "They're happy with us being here. A neighbor came up to us one day and said, 'You know, your house always looked so lonesome before you started fixing it up. Now it looks happy.'"

In this instance, we are glad to share a haunted house story with a happy ending. But then, not every homeowner is lucky enough to buy a spirited residence that comes with Casper the Friendly Ghost.

Whether you are moving into an 18th-century historic home, a newly constructed development house, a factory-manufactured mobile home or a posh, high rise apartment, don't think you are safe from the spirits. Someone who lived in that structure or who wandered on that plot of land may have committed a serious crime, or maybe a person died in the building that you now call home. There is no way to be sure of what took place before you arrived, just as there is no guarantee of what might occur after you cart in your belongings and set up house.

Sharing a Spirit

I f you're interested in witches, go to Salem, Massachusetts. However, if it's ghosts you're after, make Salem, New Jersey, your destination.

Ever since my introduction to historic Salem through Donna Robinson and her the ghost in the Richard Woodnutt House—featured in *Presence in the Parlor*—I have received several leads about haunts roaming the Garden State.

A most interesting story involves a spirited figure who appears to have settled in an impressive 18th-century structure at the northern end of Market Street, not far from Fenwick's Creek.

The half of the structure with a brick facade, featuring a plaque proclaiming the "Samuel Clement House," is owned by Ron and Diane Wohlrab. Their neighbors, whose "James Wood House" has a pale green clapboard front, is owned by Ronna Lee and Adolph "Henry" Link. Their home also is the site of Lee's Antiques.

Seated in the candle-lit cellar—also referred to as the "Tavern"—of the James Wood House, I listened to a most intriguing tale. Equally interesting, however, was the setting. The decor of the home's most popular site could easily rival any of the "reproduction" tavern-style rooms that are popular in upscale restaurants and historic towns along the East Coast. The low ceiling beams, original exposed stone walls, uneven brick floor and flaming fire from the corner hearth added to the eerie mood.

Ronna explained that the rear section of her cellar, immediately behind me, dated to the early 1700s. In another end of the room was a wooden grill, reminiscent of those found in the 18th century, above a small corner bar.

Ron and Diane started the story, explaining that on a Sunday in October a friend was in the first-floor parlor in their house, next door, tuning the strings on their harpsichord.

"He was leaning forward," Ron said, "almost done with the job, when he turned his head and looked out into the hall. There, standing only three feet from him, was a man in a great coat, in Colonial-style clothing, but without a head. Our friend said he just stared at the figure and watched it walk slowly up the stairs. Then, without letting go of the last two strings, he heard footsteps walking down the hall on the second floor."

About five minutes later, Ron added, their friend heard all kinds of noise coming from their basement, as if someone was moving chairs and boxes. The noise ended about 1:30 in the afternoon.

When Ron and Diane arrived home, their friend told them the story. Since that time, they have been watching for the headless man, but with no luck.

That was the only sighting that had ever been reported, Diane said, and they've been in the house since 1985. But, she added, both she and Ron had heard voices over the years, but the sounds never bothered them. They were more of a minor annoyance rather than something frightening.

The story, however, took a bizarre twist the next evening. On Monday night, Ron and Diane were sitting in their backyard, involved in a friendly conversation with next door neighbors Ronna and Henry.

During their informal socializing, the Wohlrabs mentioned the headless man sighting. It didn't take long for the other couple to share the rest of the story.

According to Ronna, she and Henry were entertaining another couple in their Tavern that same Sunday afternoon and evening. From about 4 o'clock to 9 that night, Ronna and Henry said, there were sounds emanating from the rear section of the cellar.

"It sounded like a gunshot, off in the distance," Henry said, "like the kind they have out in a cornfield to keep the birds away."

The snapping sounds continued throughout the evening, causing the hosts and their guests to turn involuntarily toward the muted sounds coming from darkest corners of the cellar.

After their guests left, Ronna took the stairs down into the Tavern to check on the fire.

"I turned and saw a man in a great coat, it was gray, standing in the corner of the cellar with no head!" she said, pointing to the area where the sighting occurred. "I couldn't get up the stairs fast enough. I went into the bedroom and told my husband, 'I'm not having a good night right now.' "

When she was through explaining what she saw, Henry was elected to descend to the cellar to check on the hearth and the haunt. He didn't see anything, but he admitted that he didn't spend too much time roaming the bowels of the building.

"My blood was definitely cold when I reached the top of the cellar steps," Henry said. "I couldn't shut that damper fast enough!"

"I swear it wasn't my imagination," said Ronna. "I saw a man in a coat with a cape. It was definitely gray, and he had no head. Ever since, it hasn't been as comfortable down here. I've felt the presence of a woman ever since we moved in. Now, when I come down here, I feel there's someone, or something, with me."

The two couples laughed nervously as they recalled the circumstances when they shared the stories of their common headless resident.

As Ronna said, "When Ron and Diane were telling us that their ghost had a great coat and no head, that freaked me out. And neither of us knew about what had happened in the other's house."

Ron said he found the timing of the activity significant. The last noise heard in the Wohlrab house occurred in their basement around 2 o'clock. The gunshot sounds from the back of Ronna's and Henry's cellar started two hours later.

An accidental inquiry on Halloween night may have provided the answer to mystery.

Henry said he and Ronna were at friend's home across the street where the host's son was playing with a Ouija board. Taking a chance, Henry asked the board:

Do we have a ghost?

"Yes."

Is it friendly?

"Yes."

Is it in our basement?

"Yes."

What is his name?

"Edgar Vaughn."

When did he die?

"1847"

How did he die?

"Shot his head off accidentally!"

Where in the basement?

"In the rear room."

"My next step," Henry said, "is to go to the historical society and look up Edgar Vaughn. But I certainly got a chill when I got those answers off the board."

That mid October afternoon and evening were the only two appearances of the mysterious Edgar Vaughn. Ron and Diane, who had been out when the ghost walked their halls and basement said they would love to see him "in person."

Before Christmas they tried to recreate the 1780s period, with guests in period costume, harpsichord music and candlelight.

"We tried to turn back the hands of time, to make the setting receptive for Edgar," Ron said. "But there was no sighting. We would love to repeat it. We tried hard enough."

Unfortunately, many have tried to summon the spirits and few have been successful. Just like Lady Luck, Edgar may or may not appear again.

"Maybe Edgar wanted to let someone know he existed and he's moved on," Lee said.

And then, maybe he's still in the area, waiting to make another cameo appearance in a new cellar or hallway on Market Street in Salem, New Jersey, home of a host of historic ghosts.

Conversation with 'Wolfman Jim'

T his story happened near the water, but it occurred far from Delmarva. The events took place in Maine, but it's so inter- esting, so unusual, so delightfully bizarre, that it deserves to be told—and, it happened to my son, Mark, a native Delmarvan.

In the summer of 1997, Mark, 22, who was an environmental science major at the University of Delaware, was working for a canoe company in northern Delaware.

He did a little of everything, guiding canoe trips on the nearby Brandywine River and doing maintenance on some of the equipment.

In August, his boss sent four guys in trucks up to Old Town, Maine, located on the Penobscot River, to pick up a dozen canoes and haul them back to Delaware. When they arrived, half of the order was ready, the rest of the canoes would be completed in a few days. The owner told Mark and his friend, Ken, to stay and wait for the second half of the order to be completed.

After checking into a roadside motel in Orono, the adventur- ous Delaware Duo decided to see the sights and stopped into a small bar on the side of the road.

It didn't take long for them to feel at home, settle in with a few brews and start talking to some of the regulars who came and went as the evening passed.

"We were there for a while," Mark said. "Then, this guy, Jim, who was sitting alone at a table waved us over. We both sat down

66

and he started talking, general stuff, nothing specific. He seemed okay, looked like a lot of the workers up there."

Mark said the talker had blue/gray eyes, large muttonchop sideburns and curly dark brown hair that hung onto his back well below his neck. He wore jeans and a button-down shirt. Jim said he was from New York City, and had come up for a conference being conducted at the University of Maine campus, which was located nearby.

"Everything was going fine," Mark recalled, "until Jim looked at us and calmly said, 'Satan is inside my computer.' That made us pause a minute, but we sort of ignored the comment and let it go. After all, the guy had been there for a while and he probably had a bit more to drink than we did. But, a few minutes later, he stopped in mid sentence and asked us if we believed in aliens. That gave us another reason to begin thinking that Jim might not be all there.

"When I said anything was possible," Mark said, "he was off and running. He started describing these little gray men, dressed in children's sizes because regular human adult clothing is too big for them. Jim said that different alien groups, or classes, come to Earth on a rotation schedule every day, arriving from the motherships. In the big cities, like New York, they stay in the old sewer systems and bar hop through a network of underground clubs to pick up Earth women and take them back to the ship to have children.

"I admit that at first Jim was entertaining. But the longer he talked, the more uncomfortable I got—mainly because this guy wasn't joking. He was totally serious!"

When Mark and Ken didn't seem to get involved in the little gray men conversation, Jim changed his approach.

"We were all watching something on the bar TV," Mark said, "sort of ignoring him and hoping he'd get up and leave when he asked if we believed in werewolves. I said, 'I don't know,' and Ken just looked at me oddly and tossed a real quick rolling eyeball at Jim.

"Then the guy changed the subject again, back to composting and canoes and backpacking. But soon he brought up the were-wolves again. He said a werewolf could outrun a speeding police car, jump a 12-foot fence and skin a large dog to the bone in less than a minute. He said he had taken a course on lycanthropy in some psychic center one summer," Mark added. "Then he started giving us the names of famous werewolves in history, and the towns where there had been sightings in the last 20 years."

67

Sitting in my office, listening to my son, I interrupted him. Certainly aware of my interest in things that go bump in the night, I began to get the feeling he was teasing me. "Listen, Mark," I said, sternly, "are you playing with my mind?"

"No, Dad, seriously, this is true," he said, expecting my response. "I can get Ken in here and he'll tell you the same thing."

Happily surprised, I took out a pad, urged him to continue the story and began taking notes.

As time passed that night in the bar in Orono, Jim's conversation moved toward other bizarre topics, including worm-like space creatures and Bigfoot tracks on the Appalachian Trail. Later in the evening, Mark returned from the men's room, approached the table and shouted, "Okay, Jim, let's hear about those werewolves, now!"

Immediately Jim lowered his head, motioned for quiet and whispered that there were several of *them* sitting in the bar.

Mark and Ken looked around and then slowly leaned forward to hear the rest of the story.

"I admit I'm a bit unusual," Jim told them. "Sometimes, I go out in the middle of the night in my yard and howl at the full moon, eat my meat rare, 'cause I like the taste of blood. That doesn't make me a werewolf, understand?"

Mark and Ken nodded.

"But, maybe I have werewolf tendencies," Jim said. "I don't know. Who knows about these things? All I know is what happened last night, and that I can tell you about."

Very late, near midnight the previous evening, Jim explained that he had met a number of people in the very same bar and they invited him to a party in an old Victorian house in the center of town.

"I went along," Jim told Mark and Ken. "There were about 50 people in this huge house, roaming around, drinking red wine, beer. Everything was free. I was having a good time. After a while, I wandered from the main room, the Alpha Room they called it, and I explored the rear of the home. There was a pantry, kitchen, study. It was really nice. Tall shelves built into the walls with books and antiques all over.

"After a while, I noticed I was back there all alone and no one else was around. I heard murmuring, chanting, coming from the main front rooms of the home. With my drink in hand, I walked back through about three rooms and came upon a large group of people, all dressed in similar long black robes, with hoods over their heads."

Jim paused to take a drink and looked from side to side around the bar.

Mark took a break from telling me the story and said, "Honest, Dad, this guy was weird. And my friend Ken is kicking me under the table. I was going to leave, but I thought, *God! My Dad would love this.* So I stayed. But it was getting so scary that every time Jim moved his head back and forth I thought his face was going to be a wolf's head when he turned back to face us."

Mark picked up the story and said Jim looked across the table and whispered, "You're going to find this next part amazing. As they saw me enter the room, they parted the circle and I was drawn further into the room, until I was standing in the center. The room smelled like the stench of death. It was horrible. I could hardly breathe and I tried to cover my nose to keep out the smell.

"Then, at the same time, they took off their hoods, and all their heads looked like wolves. I swear, there were black, furry, wolf heads on all of them. Then they laughed at me. It sounded like people laughter, but they looked like animals. I was freaked. I mean, this was worse than any acid trip I had ever been on.

"I dropped the wine glass and backed out of the Alpha Room and made it to the door. They all were pointing at me when I left. Some were howling, most were laughing. It was horrible. I was scared to death."

When Jim stopped, Mark and Ken exchanged looks and took a sip from their beer glasses.

It was silent. No one knew what to say.

Then Jim dropped the bomb. "You guys want to go there? I can take you there right now. Tonight!"

They boys still don't know why they followed him, maybe it was the beer, or Jim's excitement, or the young male's desire to roam and experience danger and excitement—like a wolf on the prowl.

In a few moments, Mark and Ken found themselves standing with Jim at the curb of a large white and blue Victorian home, facing a quiet, tree lined street.

It was after midnight and the neighborhood was dead. There was a light on in the back of the home, its glow hitting the back yard. Jim said he would go around to the rear and see if he could get them inside.

When he left, Ken tried to convince Mark to leave. They had had more than enough bizarre conversation and experiences for one night, he said. Mark paused, then agreed. After all, he admitted that he definitely didn't want to go into the house with Jim—and neither did Ken.

Their night on the town was approaching nightmare status and it was time to go.

Only about five minutes had passed since their wolf guide had left them. Together, Mark and Ken turned to leave before Jim came back. But, after only taking three steps away from the house, they heard a mournful howl. Turning, they saw the face of a lone wolf—or maybe it was a black and gray German Shepherd Who could be sure?

Its long snout and piercing yellow eyes were staring out the front door window. Frantically, its paws were scratching against the inside of the old wooden door, trying to get out.

Mark and Ken broke into a full run, jumped into their truck and headed back to their motel.

"We locked the door and were afraid we might have been followed," Mark said, adding that they didn't sleep very well that night.

The next morning they picked up their canoes and headed home—without stopping for a quick one at the roadside bar by the side of the Penobscot River.

Pick a Pattern

After presenting a storytelling program on the Eastern Shore, a librarian told me an interesting story about an old sea captain's home in Maine.

A retired Maryland couple—Stan and Irene—bought a second home in New England overlooking the water in a small fishing town. According to neighbors and local real estate agent, the building had been the residence of an old sea captain.

Immediately after moving in, Stan and Irene had all of the rooms decorated with either new paint or wallpaper. That included the sea captain's "den" that overlooked the coastline, even though the walls and paper were in excellent condition.

The morning after the entire house was completed, they entered the den and found strips of wallpaper ripped away from a section on two of the room's walls. The newly installed paper was dangling in long, thin shreds from the area where the walls meet the ceiling.

They called the paper hanger, demanding that he repair the damaged sections. After looking over the walls, the workman said the problem was not the result of the glue or his work. "Someone," he said, "had deliberately ripped the new paper from the wall." After some discussion with the confused owners, the workman fixed the job for an agreed-upon fee.

Stan and Irene were upset and confused with the situation, but they were relieved that the problem was resolved so quickly. But, the following morning, different sections of paper were hanging, in the same fashion, from the two other walls in the same room.

The paperhanger said it would take several days before he could return to make more repairs. In the mean time, he suggested the couple keep their kids out of the room and lock up their step ladders.

But the owners had no children or flying pets, and they didn't own a step ladder.

Two days after the second wallpaper incident, and before the workman returned, Marge, an elderly neighbor, stopped over to offer Stan and Irene information about the town and to see how things were going. During their conversation, Irene mentioned the mysterious wallpaper problem.

"What room is it happening in?" asked Marge?

"The den."

"Ah. Captain Dan's room," the woman said, smiling slightly as she continued discussing the situation. "You know," Marge added, "the captain was very, very particular about his room. He would never let anyone in there, and he definitely never let anyone else touch any of his papers or move anything around at all. I think you're going to keep on having a problem unless you let him pick out the wallpaper."

Shocked, Irene called Stan into the room and they asked Marge what she meant.

"I mean, until Captain Dan selects the pattern he wants for that room, his favorite room, you're going to have paper falling no end. Actually, I'm surprised he hasn't started slamming doors and tossing furniture around, like he did with the last two owners."

The surprised look of the owners informed Marge that the new people had no idea their house was haunted.

"Lord, you don't know about his ghost?" Marge asked, shaking her head. "He's been roaming this house for 20 years, since he passed away. Some people claim to see him on your porch, but I don't believe that nonsense. Dan never liked to sit on the porch. If he wanted to look out on the harbor, he'd just stare out his den window. He has a perfect view from inside. That's where he still is, no doubt, to this day."

After a brief tour of the den and listening to Marge's comments, Stan and Irene agreed to give her suggestion a try. That night, they placed the wallpaper sample on the desk, with the pages open to the center of the book.

As Marge predicted, the next morning two different patterns were facing the owners, and the right-hand page of the sample book had an obvious bend at the top corner.

With a mixture of shock and relief, Irene pointed to the pattern and said, "That's the signal Marge said he would give."

Nodding his head, Stan replied, "I guess that's his favorite. If you can live with it, so can I."

When Irene nodded, Stan said, "Tell the guy to put it on the walls when he gets here."

The paper hanger was surprised and pleased to get a new job—to repaper the entire den with the same pattern that had been on the walls before.

Smith Island Specters

S mith Island is Maryland's only inhabited island accessible solely by boat. Each day, at 12:30 p.m., 365 days a year, a boat—carrying the U.S. Mail and other supplies needed for daily living—leaves the dock at the end of Main Street in Crisfield, Maryland. It and other craft in the daily caravan are bound for the small patches of land that host Smith Island's three water villages—Ewell, Rhodes Point and Tylerton.

Located 12 miles offshore and surrounded by the Chesapeake Bay, Smith Island was charted by Capt. John Smith as he sailed up the Chesapeake in 1608. Its earliest European inhabitants arrived from England in 1657. But archaeological finds show that American Indians used the island many centuries earlier for ceremonies, hunting and fishing.

Today, most of the several hundred residents are descendants of the original European settlers, and some say Smith Islanders have retained a trace of the 18th-century British dialect.

While farming was initially the island's main source of livelihood, land erosion and other factors caused the islanders to focus on making their living from the sea. Many of Smith Island's residents still work the waters of the bay, and each village has its own working dock and harbor.

✳   ✳   ✳   ✳

As I arrived on Smith, I headed to the recently completed Visitor's Center, only a quick walk from the dock at the Harborside Restaurant on Levins Creek. The center sits smack dab in the thick of things, at a crossroads near the tall steepled white church and Miss Willie's Old Store, now know as Ruke's.

If you go to Smith, you should be prepared to walk. There are privately-owned cars on the island, and occasionally you'll see them passing along crushed stone lanes that are no wider than large alleys. But movement by shank's mare is the norm for most daytrippers—unless you sign up for a bus tour that is available by one of the locals.

Jennings Evans was waiting for me when I arrived. A lifelong island resident and former waterman, he also served as president of the local watermen's association. Currently retired, Jennings calls himself an "unofficial historian." He keeps active giving tours and speaking to guests at the Visitor's Center, open from noon to 4 p.m. every day. In fact, he is the narrator of the informative video that is shown several times daily in the center.

Smith Island is rich in history, and visitors can read and learn much about its association with all aspects of the country's past— such as the Battle of the Barges during the Revolutionary War and British threats and visits during the War of 1812. There are tales of picaroons and pirates hiding out in Rhodes Point—formerly known as Rouges Point—of buried treasure in the graveyards of secluded mansions and of the storms that flooded over the entire island.

Stories of the watermen and the hazards and humor of bay life abound, but that summer afternoon I was there to talk about ghosts.

In these next few pages, as much as possible, I'll let Jennings do the talking in his distinctive relaxed and informative style.

"Every place has got a lady with her head cut off. My wife's grandfather, Edgar Brimer, he's the first one that told this story. Back then, before World War II, there was no electricity on the island, except for a few generators that some people had in the backyard. But not all families had them. Electricity didn't get here until 1949.

"Before there was any lights, there was somethin', I don't know exactly what you'd call it, but there was a mist that came up outta the marshes.

"Now these guys, they wouldn't tell you lies. They've been accused of tellin' yarns around here. But when they told you somethin' it was true and you believed it. If UFOs had been available then, you woulda believed that they saw one, 'cause they'd tell you, and that's how much dependence you put on a man's word.

"This happened on Ewell. Edgar was comin' from his sister's, from 'over the hill,' that's the west side of the church. He was headin' down the lane, toward his home, when he saw a figure in the moonlight, standin' by this tree. He saw a woman there. In those days, people were polite. So they would tip their hat or even take it off, you know? How sure he was that it was a lady, is that he said, 'Good evening, ma'am.'

"And when he looked, he said to himself, 'My God! I don't see any head on her! And I know I ain't gonna get an answer.'

"So he kinda walked briskly along. His house was only another two doors down, and he kept lookin' behind, and she was standin' there the whole time. Not gettin' any communication from her, he didn't see no point in elaboratin'. When he went around the corner and into his house she was still standin' there. And when he peeked out the window, she was still there, and he went to tell his wife.

"His wife thought he was crackin' up, and when she looked, she was gone. And Edgar went outta the house to check, and she was gone.

"But he told that for truth, and whether it was a mist or some particular gasses that come outta the marsh, we don't know. He believed he saw it, and we believe he saw somethin'.

"Now, in late 1945, Stanley Marshall said he was courtin' a girl at the time. She was Mary Ann Evans, and she was stayin' with her grandmother in an old home called Pitchcroft. It was one of the oldest settlements on Smith Island and was used to keep preachers and visitors that came for the camp meetings. It was a place to take in boarders. It had an oyster house and store and an undertaker business there over the years.

"Stanley had to walk to Pitchcroft, a kinda outta the way place, and he said he always heard stories about things. So it was kinda easy to be startled. And he said, 'I think I had been drinkin' a bit, too, before I went over there.' But not after he came out, 'cause he was there two or three hours, just courtin' a girl. And he was from Tylerton, so he left his boat down near the dock.

"After he left Pitchcroft, that's what they called it, he started kinda whistlin' as he walked down a long lane. They had this gate to keep cattle in, and he had to lift this big weight on it. It was creaky like. It was another moonlight night—always seemed to be a moonlight night. I guess you couldn't see anything if there was no light.

"Anyway, he got a walkin' a while. And just before he got to where Cap'n. Edgar saw his headless lady, Stanley looked behind him and he saw a woman. Now, this one apparently had a head. He didn't look too closely, but he thought it was a bit strange for her to be out there alone at night.

"So he started to speed up his walk, thinkin' whoever it was would go into the next house or stop to meet somebody. So anyway, he walked along. He kept lookin' back, and it looked like she was gainin' on him. And he looked at her feet, and it looked like she was floatin' along.

"So he told this for the God's truth, you know? And I believed him. I was a kid when he told it to me.

"He said he started speedin' up, not quite a run, but he had a long ways to go to his boat. As he speeded up, she tiptoed along behind him. He said, 'The chills are goin' up my back.' And he told me, 'I'da liked to know for sure what it was, but in another way it was so ghastly looking that I was afraid, so I just kept on speedin' up. If I get down to the boat and she's still with me, I don't know what I'll do. Jump overboard, I guess.'

"He said when he got near to the graveyard, there wasn't nothing to do but break into a run as hard as he could go. The last he saw, she was steadily gainin' on him, but then she went behind an old confectionery stand that used to be there, and that's the last he saw of her.

"He said, 'The sweat was pourin' off of me. I'll never forget it as long as I live.' He just left us with that mystery, and he always swore it was true. And I believed him. Stanley Marshall. He died about 10 years ago.

"There also were stories about a headless woman carryin' her head in her hand. I heard different versions. Cap'n. Edgar told me himself, and I knew he weren't just tryin' to scare me.

"The way it used to be, all these old men would get up at the store there and they would talk about different things. And somebody would mention a ghost from way back. It would become a subject and they'd start to elaborate.

"You had to sort them out. But when people like Edgar told you something, you more or less believed it. What I hated about it though, I had to go home by myself. But I had a choice of goin' home and not hearin' no more conversation, or stayin' there and gettin' the pants scared off ya. And at night, I had to go over the hill, and there weren't no light except lightning bugs. Sometimes there were these green lights, the marsh is full of 'em. That's the only light I had. Sometimes I'd break into a run, imagination runnin' away with me."

On the boat ride over to Smith Island, I told Jennings I had met Gene Somers, who said that "Electric lights messed up all the ghosts."

Jennings agreed, saying there seemed to be more sightings and ghost stories before lighting arrived on the island. Then Jennings recalled another story, this one a sighting by Dr. William Stout, a semi-retired doctor that came over to live on Smith.

"Dr. Stout went down the road to Rhodes Point and said he saw this image. It kinda rose outta the marsh. He thought to himself, 'I don't believe in ghosts.' But it just amazed him how that formed right in front of his eyes.

"With it bein' in the marsh, he didn't want to take the chance to go out to it and sink up to his ears in mud. But he stood there and watched it for a while. And, all of the sudden, it started to disappear, kinda break up.

"See, he was tryin' to analyze the ghost that people was seein' around here. From his assessment of it, he thought it was some kinda marsh gas that rose up, and he knew all the people weren't lyin'. But he was brave enough to see what it was, and that was his conclusion—that the marsh sometimes puts out some kinda gas and made a form that resembled a fella with a sheet on, or whatever. It made some sense, too.

"And some people claim they seen flyin' saucers. That's another story . . . ."

For another time.

The Last Chance

I don't care what you say, boy," T.J. shouted to the weary-eyed bartender, "if I say I saw it, then I saw it! And you can take that longneck beer bottle and shove it up there where the sun don't shine!"

Ned had worked a double shift at the Last Chance, one of Rehoboth's out-of-the-way ginmills that catered to the locals throughout the year. It was a cold February night, or morning, actually. Above the back bar, the glowing Budweiser clock that was hanging out of the fish's mouth silently declared 1:30 in the morning. As usual on Tuesdays—and Wednesdays and Thursdays—T.J. was the last to leave. More times than not, Ned had to shove the drunken junk collector out into the street, and tonight was no exception.

The steady patron had nursed his final draft since he ordered it at 12:58. No matter how drunk T.J. was, Ned thought, the old guy always seemed to get that last drink in before the 1 o'clock cutoff.

"Look, T.J., my man, I didn't mean anything by it," Ned said, trying one final time to explain himself. "I only meant if you say you saw a mermaid off Cape Henlopen, it sounds a little strange. I didn't say you were ly . . . ."

"Hell with you and the ship you sailed in on!" T. J. snapped, as he stood up with substantial effort, pushed back from the bar with both hands and staggered toward the door.

"*Thank you, God*," Ned whispered, praying that nothing would stop T.J.'s advance toward the worn wooden door under the red exit sign.

Controlling his urge to offer a friendly shout of farewell, Ned raced behind T.J. and shoved the latch, locking the door.

It didn't take him long to clean up. After all, on a weeknight in late winter, Rehoboth Beach was a certifiable ghost town. Ned counted a grand total of 10 customers the entire 15 hours he had spent in the saloon. That's less than one an hour, and during the last 240 minutes it had been just him and T.J. Muggins.

Ned liked the old scavenger, usually. But when it was time to close and T.J. made it difficult, Ned had to exercise extreme control. A former school teacher, Ned had exited the classroom scene three years ago. He did not think fondly on the six long years right out of college when he had played babysitter to a never-ending stream of middle school gangsters in inner city Wilmington.

One afternoon in the middle of the school year, Ned walked out of the building during his lunch hour and never looked back. He knew he would never need another reference to re-enter the teaching profession. Since he was unmarried with no responsibilities and no car or house payments, Ned headed for the beach and fell into his current job. Since then, his life had been uncomplicated: serving up beers, listening to the same old stories and smiling and acting interested.

The heavy stream of summer tips gave him enough income to make it through the lean winters as long as he was careful. Someday he would settle down, find the right girl and right job. But, right now he had a boss who never showed up and phoned occasionally to check up on things. The Last Chance was pretty much his show. At 31, and with no personal attachments and no serious financial pressure, Ned was relatively happy.

After locking up the stock, sweeping the floor and checking the lights and locks, he paused to have a quiet beer for the road. Ned laughed, since his apartment was located right behind the bar, he could treat himself to a brewski. Hell, if he wanted, he could drink himself into oblivion and never worry about driving drunk.

His mind drifted to T.J. The old guy, who must be close to 70, had been collecting driftwood for years. Ned constantly saw the old salt—dressed in a dirty, white sea captain's cap, tan pants and a Hawaiian style shirt—hauling his planks and wood scraps into local art studios and gift shops. The owners paid him a pittance for his finds and then sold the treasured, waterworn wood to eager artists for a much higher price. But T.J. didn't care, all he wanted was enough money to buy shots and beers to go along with his daily diet of sandwiches and bar snacks.

He lived in a shack filled with junk and old sea scrap off one of the back roads towards Millsboro. Ned had been there a few times and was amazed at the accumulation of strange and apparently useless things that filled T.J.'s house, shed and small barn.

One afternoon in the Last Chance, T.J. tried to explain that he was in touch with aliens—the grays, the little three-foot fellows with almond-shaped eyes. They had selected him as a messenger, since he knew the sea. That's where they were, he told Ned, under the water, right off of Dewey. And they were going to come up and land on the beach.

A few years ago. T.J. said he had been abducted, but they brought him back with orders to let the town know that his alien friends were going to land on the sand in front of the Rehoboth Bandstand at noon on Independence Day. No one believed him and the newspapers ignored his press release. Determined to spread the word, he walked up and down the boardwalk for a week before the coming wearing a sandwich board proclaiming: "They're coming soon! Clear the sand! Prepare yourself!"

When no one moved from the prime sand location on the appointed day, T.J. took to the beach landing zone threatening bathers and sun worshipers who had planted themselves in his restricted zone. The police hauled T.J. away and gave him a three-day complimentary stay in the clink, making sure he wasn't released until the summer weekend celebration had passed.

The chief of police wasn't moved when T.J. explained that since the crew didn't arrive on July 4 they wouldn't be coming back until Labor Day weekend. The police, mayor and merchants felt much better knowing T.J. Muggins was safely out of the way temporarily.

With the load T.J. tied on, God knows how the sailor got home some nights. But, Ned thought, that wasn't his problem. Finished with his nightcap, he buttoned up his dark blue, quilted coat and pulled the hood over his head. Prepared for the blast of wind that would come off the beach, he opened the door, went outside, closed it tightly and turned the locks with his keys. Rather than taking the wooden stairs to his ground-level, three-room suite, Ned decided to take a walk on the boards.

It was just past 2 o'clock. The wind was blowing, but it wasn't as bitter as he expected. He headed for Rehoboth Avenue, walked to the end where it met the boardwalk and headed north. Pausing periodically, Ned looked out at the black sea. Only the lights of the slowly moving ships heading up toward the bay could be seen in the distance. He stopped at the edge of the wooden walkway beneath a Victorian lamplight of the Boardwalk Plaza Hotel. Turning around, he headed south and took a seat on a bench near the Atlantic Sands.

Ned was alone, and for that brief moment he owned the town.

How he would have loved to share this quiet time with someone special. The clean wind, the smell of salt water, the rhythmic splashing of the waves onto the shore. Everyone should have this experience, Ned thought. He smiled as he compared the calmness of his life—and the loneliness—to his hectic, rat-race days in the city.

It was late and he leaned his head back, closed his eyes and tried to make his mind go blank. In a moment it was just him and the sea. No one and nothing else.

Except the whimper.

Like a dog, whining for attention.

Ned opened his eyes and set his head straight ahead.

Again it sounded, the high-pitched cry from nearby.

Ned stood up. His eyes scanned the beach. The lights of the nearby streets extended his vision only so far. Standing still, he listened, waited, watched.

It didn't take long, only about 15 seconds, for it to happen again.

Ned jumped over the side of the boardwalk and landed in the sand. As he hit the beach, he heard a startled sound behind him. Turning, he saw a dark mass cramped under the boardwalk, resting on an elevated mound of sand. Stepping toward the figure, Ned saw the two eyes of an animal . . . a seal.

The brown, furry creature, huddled in what seemed to be fear and pain, stared back at Ned, who was only about 10 feet away.

Carefully, he approached the creature, which seemed to retreat as best it could from his advance.

God! Ned thought, *What am I going to do? Call the cops? Get a vet over here?*

Before he could think any further, the animal whispered, 'No."

"What?" Ned asked, looking at the strange creature.

"No," it said again, it's voice soft, like that of a young boy or girl.

"You . . . . You can talk?" Ned stammered, kneeling down and leaning the top of his body toward the animal.

"Not much," the seal said, "but enough to stop you from calling strangers here."

"You can read my thoughts?" Ned asked, feeling embarrassed that he was talking to an animal.

"Yes," the seal said, "and if you take me to strangers, they'll put me in a zoo or send me out to sea far away from my family. I need your help to get back. Look," the animal said as it pulled out its left flipper and stretched it toward Ned.

"God!" he said, seeing the oversized, deep-sea fish hook that was protruding through the seal's limb. Blood was still seeping from the wound, and the animal whined in pain as it moved the wounded limb.

"What can I do?" Ned asked, speaking nervously, and doing so softly. He still wasn't sure if the experience was real or a nightmare from the quick two beers he had polished off at the end of the night.

"Take me with you. I need some time to rest up, repair my wound and then you can lead me back into the sea."

"How can I get you to my place. I can't carry you."

"Put me in your coat and drag me down the sand. That will get me near enough, then you can hold me as you pull me along. I can still move with my other limbs."

Shaking his head, Ned spread his coat on the sand and guided the seal forward. Together, they moved down the beach in the direction of his apartment in the rear of the Last Chance. With quite a bit of effort, the odd couple made it into Ned's apartment. Quickly, following the seal's directions, he helped the animal into his bathtub and turned on the water.

As soon as the seal got settled in the bathtub, it seemed to pass out. When it did not respond to Ned's shouts or his prodding, he freaked out. Not knowing what to do next, Ned thought of the one person who could help him and the seal—T.J. Muggins.

He left the strange sea visitor in his tub and headed toward T.J.'s. Frantic, Ned woke up the old salt, dragged him into the still running car and drove the town drunk back toward town.

"What's the occasion, old buddy? You wanna kiss and make up?" T.J. slurred. His words were one long string of syllables with no separation that drifted off into the great beyond.

"You'll see when we get there," said Ned, shaking his head and wishing he had gone straight to bed.

As they entered the bathroom of Ned's castle, T.J. paused and grabbed at the wall for support. "Holy Mother of God!" he whispered. The seal was still in the tub, but obviously not doing well.

"What kinda water is that?" T.J. snapped. The sight of the sea creature had been more sobering than 10 cups of hot black coffee.

"Water, water!" said Ned. "Outta the tub!"

"Hell!" snarled T.J. "We gotta get us some sea water and fast. Quick, boy, get us some buckets and let's git us to the beach."

Grabbing a large ice tub that was used in the bar to cool kegs, T.J. and Ned raced down to the ocean and filled the trough up with salt water. When they came back, they emptied the tub and tossed the contents of the trough on top of the whining seal.

Waking up, the seal said to Ned, "That's much better."

"Good," he replied, shaking his head and still not believing the entire crazy scene.

T.J. stared at them both, not knowing what was going on. "Who ya talkin' to, boy?" he snapped.

"The seal," Ned said. "Didn't you hear it?"

"I ain't heard nothin', and I think you're nuts if ya think ya did!"

"Honest, I can hear it. It talks to me and it tells me what to do. Did that when I found it."

"Hell, don't matter to me," T.J. said, shrugging his shoulders. "She wantsa talk to you and not to me, fine. Let's just get 'er fixed on up. Lookit that there flipper, boy."

The blood was turning the water a light pink, and T.J. started to give directions.

Ned suggested getting a doctor or a vet, instead.

"Oh, sure. Let's git us a doctor in here, boy. After they grind this here bleedin' seal into fresh dog food, they'll be puttin' you and me in the funny farm for sure. Whatta you, an idiot? I ain't lettin' nobody else in on this. We'll fix 'er up and then we'll turn 'er loose. I done cut out a hellava lotta hooks in my day, and I can sure as hell do this one here. Child's play for old T.J. Muggins. Now, get me some pliers and a hacksaw. Some eye-odine, too, and a good size needle and any kinda thread. Mov'it now, boy!"

During the next hour, in a small bathroom one block from the Rehoboth Beach boardwalk, an old drunken sailor and a visibly shaken young bartender operated on an injured talking seal in a bathtub filled with grimy beach water.

As dawn approached, T.J. and Ned had brought a second fresh load of seawater into the apartment and freshened up their guest's temporary accommodations.

Exhausted, Ned sat at the kitchen table as T.J. poured them both hot coffee spiked with ginger brandy.

"Hell, boy, that was some undertakin'. I can't hardly believe it all myself, and I was right here."

"Great," Ned said, "I've got a talking seal in my apartment and a certified sea surgeon as well. So, how long do I keep your whiskered patient before I toss it back into the sea?"

" 'er," T.J. corrected him softly.

"Her?" Ned inquired.

"It's a 'er," T.J. explained, "so be polite and watch your damn language."

"Sorry," Ned said, "how can you tell?"

"Sailors know this kinda stuff. Trust me, boy," T.J. replied, obviously loving his dominant role in the current emergency seal scene. "Now, here's what we're to do. Feed 'er a good size load of fish for about three days, an' change the water twice a day. Then, by the weekend, we can toss 'er back into the water an' she should be fine. And I'll come back over and help you. No sense you druggin' her to the water alone. Okay?"

"Great. Until then I'll babysit the Creature from the Under the Boardwalk and make daily trips to the fish market. I bet this place is going to smell like a dock."

"Hey," T.J. said, "I'll take care of the damn fish deliveries. You just run in a few times every day and check on 'er and change the bandages an' water, regular. All right?"

Ned agreed, and for the next three days he found himself spending more and more time inside the bathroom with his guest—but he did so willingly.

He learned that her name was Morra. Her family of seals was from Nova Scotia, and each year they traveled the Atlantic Coast, swimming in herds of up to 300. Since they never came near sight of shore they were rarely seen by humans.Swimming only at night they were usually safe, but a massive deadly hook, floating swiftly below the surface from a deep sea charter boat hooked her left limb. As she was being pulled away the herd, her father and brothers tried to chew on the line and set her free. But the fisherman had set the hook too well, and nothing could help her. As the motor of the boat pulled her away in the opposite direction, she saw fear and sadness in the eyes of her family. But they were helpless. There was nothing they could do.

It had happened before, she explained, to others. She was not the first to be caught. Luckily, she was able to chew through the nylon cable, break free and swim off and make it to shore without being seen. Maybe someday she would catch up with the herd. But it will be hard to swim the long journey alone and reach them.

Ned noticed that he began to look forward to the visits. Nightly, after closing, he sat on the edge of the bathtub and talked for hours. He told Morra about his short teaching career, about his desire to become a painter, and how sometimes it bothered him to be alone.

The conversations were comfortable. They spoke as if they were two old friends sharing common experiences. Sometimes, they sat in silence, not speaking at all, but it felt good.

She explained the colony and how they raced through the water, seeing the underside of the ocean that man had never touched. She described the unspoiled colors of the sea floor, the sunken ships and treasures they passed, the delicate ocean life that existed in its deepest depths.

When she spoke, he sensed the freedom of movement, the lack of pressure, the sense of real living that still existed in her world.

Without enthusiasm, he told her of the hectic life on land, of housing developments, business pressures and stress, of the never ending quest for money and property, clothing and objects—things that eventually would be left behind, discarded and sold.

He tried to explain the concept of rent and bills. He dared not discuss taxes and religion, race and politics. Ned realized they would have been too complex and absurd to share.

"Why do humans do it?" Morra asked, innocently. "Why do they tie themselves down to one place and work for so long in unhappy settings? It sounds like you trade your lifetime to exist not live, and all most people receive is two weeks of rushed vacations that are anything but enjoyable."

Ned smiled. "I agree. When I try to explain my world to you it sounds almost absurd. Sometimes, I wish I could go away, to a better place. But there is no better place. There's only here for me. And whether it's Rehoboth or Cape Cod or California or Maine, it's still a rat-race for money and scratching out an existence. But," he said, forcing a weak smile, "that's life. There's no way around it. But I don't have it so bad, at least I can tend bar and I'm not in school anymore. That was hell beyond compare."

"But," Morra asked, "is what you have now good or only less bad?"

Ned stared at the seal in the tub and wouldn't reply. He knew the answer. He knew that his life was just a series of lesser degrees of disappointment. His present situation was nothing to be thrilled with, and it would soon grow old. As he fell asleep later that night, he realized that he was talking about degrees of unhappiness, and that realization was depressing.

For a moment he wished he could disappear into the water beside her when she left, swim away from life as he knew it. But that thought was as absurd as his entire week.

Every few hours for the next few days, Ned changed the dressing and applied salve to the wounded limb. He flinched the first time he saw the horrible stitching job that amateur doctor T.J. had performed on the seal's flipper. A wide scar was forming.

"Hey," T.J. snapped when Ned complained, "This ain't no fancy 'E.R.' or 'Chicago Hope,' boy. I got 'er sewed up so she wouldn't bleed on outta here. What more do ya want, blood?" With that the sailor let out a belly laugh, satisfied with his own accidental joke.

When the fourth day came, the amateur medics decided Morra needed a bit more time to recuperate. Ned and T.J. changed the water for five more days. But after more than a week of recuperation, it was time return Morra to sea.

At 2:30 on an early March morning when the beach was deserted, the two men dragged a carpet from the apartment in the rear of the Last Chance. Silently, they pulled the rug down a side street, across the boardwalk and onto the sand.

As the seal smelled the surf, she scampered excitedly off the carpet and raced toward the water. Slowly, she moved along the damp sand, leaving marks on the beach sand.

Then, more quickly, she pranced along the edge of the crashing waves and white surf.

Ned and T.J. smiled while Morra tested her mended limb. As she applied pressure, she could sense it was strong. It was fixed well enough to swim without fear or concern.

"Thank you both!" she called back. Her voice carried over the sounds of the sea.

"You're welcome," Ned said, waving back. Tears began filling up the base of his eyes.

"Not a bad job, eh?" T.J. said, pointing to his surgery repair job in action. "Well, let's get back in an' git us a drink. She's gotta go, and you standing here ain't gonna make it easy on none of us. Come on, boy," T.J. ordered.

Before he could turn away, the seal called out, "Ned, remember, strange things happen for a reason!"

"Right!" he shouted back. His voice cracked as he watched her disappear in the surf.

T.J. was already climbing the steps to the Boardwalk, but Ned stared at the ocean, hoping to catch a last glimpse of the special friend he would never see again.

That next summer, Ned bought an easel and set it up on the beach. He spent a few hours three times a week in less traveled portions of Cape Henlopen. Often, Ned would see T.J. Muggins scrounging for driftwood along the beach.

Sometimes, the old sailor would drop down on the sand and spend and hour or two in conversation. The conversation would be continuations of the previous night's debate in the Last Chance or they would include topics that interested the old buccaneer—UFOs, alien abductions, Bigfoot sightings, sunken treasure, long distance rates, pirate ghosts and assorted government conspiracies.

Ned was amazed at T.J.'s wide range of knowledge. And, yes, often they would talk about the seal.

"Ya know, boy," T.J. said, "there's some days I don't believe it happened. An' other days, I'm so sure that I look out on the water an' hope to see 'er come right out at me. Ya know what I mean?"

Ned nodded. "Yeah," he said, pausing. "I don't know why it was us, T.J. I mean, it could have been anybody else there that night, or somebody could have spotted her earlier in the day. Why us?"

" 'Cause she could trust us. That's why. Some other yahoo woulda called the paper to git their name in lights and put 'er in a zoo and said who cares. But we done the right thing, boy. Done it correctly, as far as I see it. Ya know?"

"Yeah, I know," Ned agreed. "But there was so much more I wanted to know, to hear about, to say to her. I really enjoyed talking to her. Does that sound crazy to you?"

T.J. let out a roar, and Ned answered his own question. "God! What am I saying? Nothing sounds crazy to you."

It was in early fall, during a weekday afternoon, when Ned was seated with his easel on the sand. No one had passed by for hours, and he had just about completed his favorite painting. T.J. was going to come by and pick him up in time to get to work.

Ned stood up, stepped back and looked at the artwork. It was unusual, but, he thought, magnificent. Coming out of a round seashell, similar to a cornucopia featured in drawings during Thanksgiving, was a stream of water. In the front, where the flow was the widest, was a beautiful mermaid. Her hair was golden yellow, her flesh smooth and pale. At the bottom of her body was one large brown fin instead of legs.

The mermaid's brown eyes were very expressive, staring straight out of the painting, as if they were focused on the artist or the person viewing the work.

As he began to pack up his materials, a shadow formed behind him. He turned to see a woman with dark flowing hair, long legs and the athletic body of a swimmer.

"May I look?" she said. She held tightly to a large white towel that was wrapped around her shoulders.

"Sure," Ned said, looking around for a car or some sign of how she had arrived.

"Very nice," she said.

"Thanks," Ned said. "I've been working on it for some time now."

"Does it have a name?"

"No, not yet," he said, "but I've got an idea or two."

"Can I make a suggestion?" she asked.

"Why not?" Ned said, smiling, noticing something familiar about the woman.

"I'd call it 'Morra.' "

Ned froze and stared, not at her face, but at the left hand that was reaching to take his. Her hand was soft, but her forearm was scarred above the wrist.

"I've been waiting for you," he said.

"I know," she replied, smiling. "I came as quickly as I could. Now that I'm here there's only one question: Your world or mine? We only get one chance, and we have to choose now."

"I decided that the minute you left," Ned said. "Take me with you."

Slowly, as the young couple walked toward the sea, T.J. arrived in his four-wheel pickup. He walked to the painting and stopped. A hundred yards away, at the water's edge, he saw two lovers embrace and kiss on the sand. Then, ever so quickly, before his very eyes, as they walked into the water they changed into seals, both of them.

And they disappeared into the sea.

Across the top of the painting were the words:

To T.J., From Ned and Morra. Good-bye.

Watery Grave

Cleitus Abnor sat on his back porch, rocking in an old wooden chair and puffing on a briar pipe filled with cherry blend tobacco. There was a slight breeze, barely enough to stir the dry leaves and move the rising smoke during that summer evening in August 1997.

A full moon lit up the flat cornfield behind his farmhouse, and a few hundred frogs were burping a low-pitched concert down at the nearby millpond. Cleitus pointed with the stem of his pipe, remarking how the fireflies looked like twinkling Christmas lights against the backdrop of the distant forest.

At 91, Cleitus' mind was still as sharp as it was 69 years ago, when he left behind his family home in Old Conowingo and moved across the Mason-Dixon line into nearby southern Pennsylvania.

We talked a while about the last days in the old town, before it was flooded over and buried in a watery grave beneath the 9,000-acre, 13-mile lake that was formed when the government dammed up the mighty Susquehanna.

Painting pictures from a reservoir of memories that had been safely tucked in his mind, Cleitus smiled as he talked about the good times—when life was simpler than today, when a man's word was his bond, when a handshake was better than a written contract.

"Ya know," he said, shaking his head, "hardly nobody remembers the old town, the real Conowingo. They think them car lots an' ginmills down on Route 1 is the place. But the real town was

flooded over, covered up with water just like that there lost conti-
nent of Atlantis."

He paused, taking another puff, and then picked up on his
thoughts. "I can still see the streets, with the church, stores, the
canneries an' our little frame house—sometimes as clear as if I
was still standing right down there. But it's been close to 70 years
since it all went away. Gone under deep water. I tell ya, I wonder
what the fish think, swimmin' through all those houses, makin'
their way through the broken winders and doors, floating in an'
outta rooms that used to be filled with people. If you think about
it, it can make you a little bit crazy. An' to people who don't know
nothin' about the floodin', they look at you like you're outta your
mind if ya mention it."

It was on January 18, 1928, when Old Conowingo was evacuat-
ed and its residents were paid to relocate. The 100-foot-high dam
across the Susquehanna River was built to provide needed electricity to the growing region. At the time, the structure was second
only to Niagara Falls in electric generating capacity.

The purpose of my visit was to hear some old folktales about
the area, to catch some of the former residents before they died
off. I had been told that an interview with Cleitus Abnor should be
at the top of my list.

The original one-hour interview extended to two, then three.
Around 11, Cleitus warmed up a pot of thick coffee that had been
on the stove for more than a day. "I brew me a big pot," he said,
"then got it done for two or three days. Nothin' like thick, black
coffee—with some of the grounds floatin' in it—to clean you out
an' get you on the run," he added.

Around about midnight my attention was starting to fade. I
put my pen in my pocket and was getting ready to head to my car
when Cleitus made an offhand comment that grabbed my attention.

"I guess you don' wanna hear about Young Charlie McDoon
an' Benny Hemp. One of them boys never made it up to the high
ground."

The look in my eyes and the eagerness on my face made
Cleitus laugh. "I can tell from the way you snapped yer head
'round that you're sorta interested."

"Yeah," I said, nodding, and reopening my notebook.

"Well, I been holding this inside me for all these years, so I guess I better get it out before I get called home. Make me feel better, I guess. Besides, all their family's gone, an' the story ain't gonna hurt nobody no how, not now."

I leaned back against the porch post, stretched my feet across the steps and listened as Cleitus told me a tale that I still find hard to believe. But that won't keep me from sharing it with you.

"Young Charlie McDoon an' Benny Hemp were best friends. I mean real good friends. Lived on the same road, hung out all the time. You'd never see one of 'em without the other."

Over the years, Cleitus said, the two boys took jobs on the river, hauling freight in open rafts, working deliveries on the docks and doing a lot of lumberin' as well. There was a big call for trees cut from the forest that lined the river in them days.

"Came to be," he said, "that in the early 1920s, the boys got caught up with some moonshiners who was working over in Harford County and up in Pennsylvania.

"That gang was a rough lot," Cleitus said, shaking his head side to side. "Mean as spit an' would kill ya as much as look at ya. Anybody in their right mind woulda stayed clear, so that's why I can't figure them two boys to get hooked up with 'em. But, I seen some strange things in my life an' their business wasn't my business, so I let it be."

The two Conowingo boys eventually were running kegs of white lightning to about a half-dozen towns along the Susquehanna, dropping off their loads at night and getting payment that was supposed to go back to the bootleggers up river.

"For almost two years, from about '26 to '28, at the same time they was workin' on buildin' the dam, they was livin' the good life. They had them fancy clothes, good lookin' women—I mean real good lookin' women—an' a fast movin' getaway car, modified for hauling booze into the backroads and gettin' away from the revenuers—ifin they would show up.

"Apparently, Benny, he got his self hooked up with some floozy by the name of Jasmine Linn. That was her stage name. See, she sang in them gin joints along the strip. So to keep the pretty young thing in her accustomed style, Benny started skimmin' some of the boss's payoff money.

"He would take 50, or a hundred or whatever, outta the envelope for his own use—without telling his partner Young Charlie," Cleitus said. "Then, he'd go out an' spend it on Jasmine, but it didn't take too long for the big boys to notice an' come after Young Charlie and Benny both.

"The moonshiners caught up with them as Benny and Young Charlie was comin' outta a beer hall near Rising Sun. Hell, them two young boys from Old Conowingo was no match for those big ol' bootleggin' boys. They was big farmers, used to carryin' hay bales an' liftin' and movin' their stills a few times a month. They just beat the blazes outta Young Charlie and Benny.

"They told 'em it was a warning an' they expected the money back. After they drove off, Benny had to tell Charlie why they got the stuff kicked outta them an' they got into a tiff 'tween the two of themselves. But they got over it an' scraped and borrowed to pay off the debt."

But, Cleitus said, "Ain't nothin' a match for the wink of a schemin' woman's eye, I tell ya. Weren't too long an' Benny was back to his theivin' ways. But this time it didn't take but one time for the moonshiners to find out.

"When he cut into their first payment, they come swoopin' down outta the woods one night an' like to killed Young Charlie with the end of a 2-by-4. Beat his brains senseless, then they cut off his right hand an' tossed it in the Susquehanna. Since he really didn't do nothin', guess he was livin' proof that you should be careful 'bout the comp'ny ya keep. They drove off in the dust with Benny in the back of a black Ford, an' left Young Charlie with one hand, screamin' and moanin' on the side of the road.

"But they did worse to Benny, 'cause they knowed he was the real fly in the pie.

"Nobody heard nothin', I mean nothin', about Benny for months. Now, Jasmine, they say she tooked up with some other fella in no time 'tall. Young Charlie was good for nothin', all gimped up and shocked to hell. They say he lost his right speech, got to be a stutterer he was so shook up and all. But wasn't a word 'bout Benny, 'til . . . ."

Cleitus paused to relight his pipe and even the sounds of nature were silent, as if they critters also were waiting to hear more in the darkness. I stared at the real-life storyteller of old, patient for the end of his tale.

"Well, 'til Jan'ary, when they closed up the new dam and' flooded the back country. Seems them moonshiners had kept Benny around as a sorta servant boy, goferin' this an' goferin' that.

Poor soul thought they was gonna forget about punishin' him an' let 'im go. But that was no way gonna happen.

"On January 18, 1928, remember the day, they shut up the gates an' started flooding the north side of the Susquehanna. Oh, there was people lining the banks from all over the county and three or four states, I tell ya. A sight to behold. While the water was backin' up on the north end, the south side was dryin' out like a bone. After a spell, ya could see the rocks down below an' couldn't see nothing but water fillin' up on the other side.

"Now, we all had to evacuate the town, Old Conowingo. We got our few possessions out days before. Then the townsfolk stood on the hill and watched for hours as the water buried their homes and streets an', why, everything just was swallowed up.

"But, back to Benny. Well, ole Moonshiner Mike, leader of the gang, took his boys down to the river's edge to watch the back fill up. He wasn't no sentimental guy, but even he figured it was to be a once in a lifetime look at things as they was never ever gonna be again.

"We drove down to see Old Conowingo go, then we hopped in our trucks and headed further up north, out of sight of the spectators. Benny, he was sittin' near me when we stopped and got out. Mike waved for us to follow, so we did. Ya didn't ignore Moonshine Mike, and ya never asked 'Why?' Ya just did, ya know?

"So, me and Benny is walkin' along, an' I'm gettin' a strange feelin'. An' it wasn't just me. A few of the other guys is sorta walkin' a little slower than usual, and nobody is sayin' nothin' about nothin' to nobody.

"Benny, he could sense the mood, an' I can seed him startin' to sweat, even though it wasn't hot. It was Jan'ary. Winter. All of a sudden, three guys jump on toppa Benny an' press 'im against the ground an' Mike is bending' over, lookin' at him, only inches from his face. Their eyes are almost touchin'. Then they drag Benny to a tree, only about 8 feet above the rising water line an' tie him to it, like them movies where Joan o' Arc is roped up to a stake.

"All the time, Benny's beggin' first, then cryin', then screamin' to be let go. He's yellin' for another chance. An' Moonshine Mike is laughin' an' slappin' him across the face. The other guys are spittin' on him an' beatin' him with sticks. Then, as all this is happenin', the water is risin', little by little. Inch by inch.

"A few of the guys are havin' beer, laughin' an' talkin' an' throwin' rocks at Benny, who's gonna drown soon, anyway. Then

Moonshine Mike says, 'Ya wanna scream? I'll give ya somethin' to scream about!' An' he started hittin' Benny real hard with his both fists, I mean one, two—one, two—over an' over, 'till Mike's hands was all bloody an' Benny's face was a real sticky red mess. We all stood there. Nobody said not a word. Nobody wanted to finish them beers after that, neither.

"Then Benny, he let out the loudest, worst scream I ever did hear. Like a wild animal caught in a trap, it was. I never heard nothin' like it, never want to hear the likes of that again. Then, Moonshine Mike got into the car an' said the party was over.

"We all left. I was one of the last ones to get in the back seat."

Cleitus stopped for a minute. He was looking off, in the distance, toward the southwest, in the direction of the Susquehanna.

"Sometimes, I still picture Benny, up against that tree, screamin' an' cryin' as the water was coverin' his ankles. He wasn't goin' nowhere, that was for sure.

"We left. Wasn't nothin' nobody could do. He musta died real bad. I imagine it woulda been better to shoot 'em. I would taken that instead of bein' drownded like that.

"I wonder what he was thinkin' when the water reached his chest, then his neck, then got up on over his mouth? What a way to go, knowin' ya couldn't do nothing—just waitin' for the river to cover ya up an' end it all."

Cleitus paused for a good while. The minutes seemed extra long that time of the morning.

Then, he looked over to me.

"I never told that to nobody. Don't rightly know why I told it to you. But I feel better now," he said. "You can write it in down in your book if ya want. Just change my name. Fair enough?"

I nodded.

"Ya know. Funny thing is, sometimes folks that make up stories about the people they say got left behind when the waters come into Old Conowingo. They say there was people who chosed t' be drownded rather than t' leave. Claim others was chained to the doors and left down there to die.

"I heard 'em all. An' I can't say if any is true, but I think not. Just tall tales to scare the kids is all. But Benny and Young Charlie. What happened to them's true. I know. I seed it all. Seed that hand fly through the air an' plop down in the water. Seed the river crawlin' up Benny's feet. Some sights, I tell ya.

"I went back only one time. To near the place where Benny disappeared. Close as I could get, ya know. But he's so far down I'd never be able to see nothin'. I knew that before I went. It had to be five, maybe even 10 years after.

"Didn't 'spect to see nothin'. Couldn't anyway. It was night. But, I say, it was ice cold there. Scary. Like death was in the air. That big lake drank up Benny, an' I bet, over the years, there's bound to be a few more tossed down there keepin' him comp'ny. I never been back since. Don't want to go. Don't need to go. Don't never plan to go. No, sir.

"I seed all I want of that Susquehanna. Old Conowingo and Benny should be left alone. People shouldn't go on a messin' where they don't not belong. No tellin' what they'd find."

Headless Horseman of Ragged Point Channel

Chincoteague Island is on the Atlantic Ocean side of the Eastern Shore of Virginia, not too far from the Maryland border. The island is home to a small fishing village and a popular resort area that is about seven miles long and one-and-a-half miles wide. The island and settlement of Chincoteague is protected from the full force of the Atlantic by Assateague Island, one of the many barrier islands along the East Coast. Assateague Island National Seashore extends approximately 37 miles from northern Virginia into southern Maryland. It offers miles of attractive unspoiled beaches and is home of the famous wild ponies.

The early colonists of Chincoteague—which in the Indian language means "Beautiful Land Across the Water"—were sailors and livestock herders who arrived in the 1670s. Their main source of income was farming, raising livestock, fishing and salvaging whatever floated onto shore from the many shipwrecks off Assateague Island.

For a time, a number of families lived and died on Assateague. Eventually, they moved off the island, many resettling on Chincoteague Island. In fact, some of the Assateague homes were transported across the bay and were used as residences on Chincoteague.

Today, however, the most famous residents of Assateague Island are the wild ponies.

According to legend, the island ponies are descendants of horses that made their way to shore in the 16th century after the

Spanish galleon they were traveling on wrecked at sea. Since that time, the ponies have lived on Assateague Island and they have attracted tourists from around the world. Each July, many thousands of visitors arrive in Chincoteague for the annual Wild Pony Round-Up, Swim and Auction.

But there are other fascinating stories and legends about Chincoteague and Assateague. Some folks tell of buried pirate gold. Others enjoy the boastful yarns of island market hunters who outfoxed pesky game wardens. And still more recall the sad stories of souls lost in turbulent seas.

Then, there's the story of the Headless Horseman of Ragged Point Channel.

Chincoteague resident David Quillen shared his version of the tale that was told to him by his grandmother many times over the years. But, he added, there are several different accounts of this story that has become an area favorite and one that has been retold and embellished over the last century.

✳   ✳   ✳   ✳

More than 100 years ago, the people on Chincoteague owned or rented land on Assateague Island where they grazed their livestock.

In the late 1800s, around 1890, a gentleman decided to head over to Assateague to check on his livestock. A storm was approaching and he wanted to make sure his animals were secure. At the time, there was little or no distance across the channel to the outer island. In some places, David said, you could practically walk across since the water wasn't that deep. But time has eroded and washed away many of the small marsh islands that used to stand in the channel.

The livestock owner's wife begged him not to go, to stay home. She was worried and pleaded for him to remain with the family and to wait until after the storm had passed.

But, the husband ignored his wife's demands, saddled his horse and rode onto Assateague Island. That night, during the storm, a bolt of lightning struck his neck and severed his head from his body.

The stormy decapitation occurred at the edge of Ragged Point Channel, on Assateague Island, across from the northern end of Chincoteague Island.

Afterward, for several years, the dead man's wife said she would go out at night and could hear the sound of hoofbeats and her husband's sad, frustrated voice, screaming as he continued to search for his head.

Even today, some believe the Headless Horseman of Ragged Point Channel still rides. If you are lucky, you can catch a glimpse of him along the coastline of Assateague, particularly during a lightning storm.

He's the fellow dressed in black, sitting atop a large, dark horse—headless, of course—and frantically searching for that most important part of his body.

But, folks say he'll be riding for a long time, and he will never, ever, find his long lost head.

About the Author

Ed Okonowicz, a Delaware native and freelance writer, is an editor and writer at the University of Delaware, where he earned a bachelor's degree in music education and a master's degree in communication.

Also a professional storyteller, Ed is a member of the National Storytelling Association. He presents programs at country inns, retirement homes, schools, libraries, private gatherings, public events. Elderhostels and theaters in the mid-Atlantic region.

He specializes in local legends and folklore of the Delaware and Chesapeake Bays, as well as topics related to the Eastern Shore of Maryland. He also writes and tells city stories, many based on his youth growing up in his family's beer garden–Adolph's Cafe–in the Browntown section of Wilmington, Delaware.

Ed presents storytelling courses and writing workshops based on his book *How to Conduct an Interview and Write an Original Story*. With his wife, Kathleen, they present a popular workshop entitled, *Self Publishing: All You Need to Know about Getting—or Not Getting—into the Business*.

About the Artist

Kathleen Burgoon Okonowicz, a watercolor artist and illustrator, is originally from Greenbelt, Maryland. She studied art in high school and college, and began focusing on realism and detail more recently under Geraldine McKeown. She enjoys taking things of the past and preserving them in her paintings.

Her first full-color, limited-edition print, *Special Places*, was released in January 1995. The painting features a stately stairway near the Brandywine River in Wilmington, Delaware.

A graduate of Salisbury State University, Kathleen earned her master's degree in professional writing from Towson State University. She is currently a marketing specialist at the International Reading Association in Newark, Delaware.

The couple resides in Fair Hill, Maryland.

For information on other titles by Ed Okonowicz,
see pages 102- 106.

A
DelMarVa
Murder
Mystery

Get FIRED!

It's early in the 21st century and DelMarVa, the newest state in the union is making headlines. There is full employment. Its residents pay no taxes. The crime rate is falling. And, with five casino-entertainment centers and a major theme park under construction, it's soon to be one of the country's top tourist destinations.

Just about everything is going right.

But, in the first year of this bold experiment in regional government, a serial kidnapper strikes . . . and the victims are a steadily growing number of DelMarVa residents.

Will the person the newspapers have dubbed "The Snatcher" ruin DelMarVa's utopian state? Or will the kidnapper be caught and swing from a noose at the end of a very stiff rope— since both hanging and the whipping post have been reinstated to eliminate crime on the peninsula.

In this first DelMarVa Murder Mystery, meet Governor Henry McDevitt, Police Commissioner Michael Pentak and state psychologist Dr. Stephanie Litera, as they pursue the peninsula's most horrifying kidnapper since the days of Patty Cannon.

ISBN 1-890690-01-5

$9.95

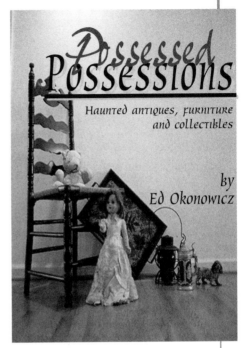

"If you're looking for an unusual gift for a collector of antiques, or enjoy haunting tales, this one's for you."
—COLLECTOR EDITIONS

" a book that will be a favorite among collectors, dealers, and fans of the supernatural alike."
—THE MIDATLANTIC ANTIQUES

". . . an intriguing read."
—MAINE ANTIQUE DIGEST

". . . a good way to relax following a long day walking an antique show or waiting at an auction. The book is certainly entertaining, and it's even a bit disturbing.
—ANTIQUEWEEK

POSSESSIONS

Haunted antiques, furniture and collectibles

by
Ed Okonowicz

A bump. A thud. Mysterious movement. Unexplained happenings. Caused by what? Venture beyond the Delmarva Peninsula and discover the answer. Experience 20 eerie, true tales, plus one horrifying fictional story, about items from across the country that, apparently, have taken on an independent **spirit** of their own–for they refuse to give up the ghost.

From Maine to Florida, from Pennsylvania to Wisconsin . . . haunted heirlooms exist among us . . . everywhere.

Read about them in **Possessed Possessions**, *the book some antique dealers definitely do not want you to buy.*

$9.95

112 pages
5 1/2 x 8 1/2 inches
softcover
ISBN 0-9643244-5-8

Available in August 1998

MORE *Possessed* Possessions **2** Haunted Antiques, Furniture and Collectibles

103

*S*pirits *Between the Bays*

Series

True
Ghost Stories
from the
master storyteller
Ed Okonowicz

Volume by volume our haunted house grows. Enter at your own risk.!

Open the door and wander through these books of true ghost stories of the Mid Atlantic region. Creep deeper and deeper into terror, until you run Down the Stairs and Out the Door in the last of our 13 volumes.

"If this collection doesn't give you a chill, check your pulse, you might be dead."
—Leslie R. McNair
The Review, University of Delaware

" 'Scary' Ed Okonowicz . . . the master of written fear— at least on the Delmarva Peninsula . . . has done it again."
—Wilmington News Journal

"This expert storyteller can even make a vanishing hitchhiker story fresh and startling. Highly Recommended!"
—Chris Woodyard
Invisible Ink: Books on Ghosts & Hauntings

See order form on page 106.